Psychological Testing
in Everyday Life

To GWM, with love

Psychological Testing in Everyday Life

History, Science, and Practice

Karen B. Goldfinger

Los Angeles | London | New Delhi
Singapore | Washington DC | Melbourne

FOR INFORMATION:

SAGE Publications, Inc.
2455 Teller Road
Thousand Oaks, California 91320
E-mail: order@sagepub.com

SAGE Publications Ltd.
1 Oliver's Yard
55 City Road
London, EC1Y 1SP
United Kingdom

SAGE Publications India Pvt. Ltd.
B 1/I 1 Mohan Cooperative Industrial Area
Mathura Road, New Delhi 110 044
India

SAGE Publications Asia-Pacific Pte. Ltd.
3 Church Street
#10–04 Samsung Hub
Singapore 049483

Printed in the United States of America

Library of Congress Cataloging-in-Publication Data

Names: Goldfinger, Karen, author.

Title: Psychological testing in everyday life : history, science, and practice / Karen B. Goldfinger.

Description: Thousand Oaks, California : SAGE, [2019] | Includes bibliographical references and index.

Identifiers: LCCN 2017048475 | ISBN 9781483319315 (pbk. : alk. paper)

Subjects: LCSH: Psychological tests—History.

Classification: LCC BF176 .G65 2019 | DDC 150.28/7—dc23
LC record available at https://lccn.loc.gov/2017048475

SFI label applies to text stock

This book is printed on acid-free paper.

Acquisitions Editor: Abbie Rickard
Editorial Assistant: Jennifer Cline
Production Editor: Nevair Kabakian
Copy Editor: Ashley Horne
Typesetter: Hurix Digital
Proofreader: Sally Jaskold
Indexer: Judy Hunt
Cover Designer: Alexa Turner
Marketing Manager: Katherine Hepburn

18 19 20 21 22 10 9 8 7 6 5 4 3 2 1

BRIEF CONTENTS

DETAILED CONTENTS

PREFACE

*P*sychological Testing in Everyday Life: History, Science, and Practice examines psychological testing in different arenas to help students become informed and thoughtful test consumers, whether they are taking a psychological test themselves or using tests to make decisions about others. It will help students who are studying psychometrics understand both the strengths and limitations of psychological tests, what tests can and cannot do.

By using examples that are meaningful to college students and a narrative approach to instruction, this book makes the study of psychometrics interesting, relevant, and easier to master than standard psychometric textbooks. The broad range of topics covered, and the depth of coverage of individual topics, ensures that most students will find something in the text they can relate to personally or professionally. In addition, the material is presented in a lively, readable, and accessible style that is engaging for college students at all levels.

After reading the text, students will have a better appreciation for core psychometric concepts because they will see their impact on decisions that affect themselves, people they know, and the world around them. They will begin to appreciate the complexities of using psychological tests in real-life situations, including the legal hurdles and technical challenges that have to be addressed.

An additional goal of the text is to engage students in critical thinking about all aspects of the testing process. The decisions that need to be made about how, when, and why to use a test are not always straightforward. Different decision makers could justify making different choices. The text aims to motivate students to think about the issues raised, and the selected material is current and compelling enough to inspire students to have ideas and points of view of their own.

The text explains the basic principles behind psychometrically sound tests and underscores, repeatedly, the importance of using psychometrically sound tests when important decisions are based on test results. After reading the text, students should have a firm understanding of the significance of psychometrics as well as an awareness of the frequent use of psychological testing in a variety of contexts.

In most courses on psychometrics, the book can be used to supplement a traditional psychometric textbook. In less technically oriented courses, the text can stand alone. Each chapter starts with learning objectives to orient students to the material in the chapter and ends with discussion and research questions to expand student learning and mastery of the chapter contents. These questions make for lively classroom discussion starters and interesting term paper topics as well.

Karen B. Goldfinger
Essex, Connecticut

ACKNOWLEDGMENTS

This book could not have been written without the support of family, friends, and colleagues. The many college students I have known personally and professionally have helped me understand what students can do and what they might need from a textbook, and the book has benefitted from those insights. I am also appreciative of the faculty at SUNY at Binghamton and SUNY at Albany who taught me the value of science many years ago. I never forgot.

I also want to thank the first editor of the book, Reid Hester, for his encouragement from the very beginning and for his help in shaping the proposal and the early stages of the book. Abbie Rickard took the reins as editor and helped tremendously in clarifying ideas, writing, and rewriting. She turned the manuscript into a textbook that will help students master the material and one that I am proud of. Finally, I want to thank the reviewers of the proposal and of the text for their careful attention and very valuable feedback. They are:

Amy Martin, Rockford University

Anne-Marie R. Iselin, University of North Carolina Wilmington

Jane L. Swanson, Southern Illinois University Carbondale

Dr. Jill S. Haasch, Elizabeth City State University

John M. Spores, Purdue University Northwest

Shannon Robertson, Jacksonville State University

ABOUT THE AUTHOR

Karen B. Goldfinger, PhD, is a licensed clinical psychologist in private practice in Connecticut. She is the lead author of a textbook on psychological assessment, *Psychological Assessment and Report Writing*, and a former adjunct faculty member for a psychology graduate program. She has a wealth of experience in psychological testing and has long been interested in when, why, where, and how psychological tests are used in everyday life.

INTRODUCTION

LEARNING OBJECTIVES

- Discuss at least five ways psychological tests contribute to decision making in everyday life
- Describe how psychological tests are used in basic and applied research
- Describe the purpose of a psychological test
- Discuss three different ways of categorizing tests
- Define the term *psychological test*

PSYCHOLOGICAL TESTING IN EVERYDAY LIFE

Janey is in 3rd grade. Her math textbook is incomprehensible to her parents, even though they attended the same school Janey goes to not that long ago. How come? Who decided to change the curriculum? At the highest levels of government, decisions about educational goals and how to reach them are made, at least in part, on the basis of results of standardized tests that are administered to a small, representative sample of students, with a goal of improving the academic performance of students as they compete with peers around the globe.

Jonah experienced complications with his birth, and as a result, he is slow to learn. His mother applied for help from the Department of Developmental Services so that she can get additional support for him. She has to submit documentation indicating that he has an intellectual disability, and Jonah has to take a test of cognitive ability, a psychological test, as part of the application process.

Hector also has to take a psychological test. He is applying for a management position in a large retail corporation. He did well on his interview but now he has to take a personality test. The employer wants to make sure he is emotionally stable and a good fit for the management team.

Harold too has to take a test. A college student, he is struggling with depression and he is not doing very well in his classes. His therapist thinks Harold might have Attention Deficit Hyperactivity Disorder (ADHD), but he isn't sure, and he referred him to a colleague for testing. He will revise the treatment plan for Harold if he has ADHD, and Harold might also be eligible for academic accommodations.

These are some examples of how psychological tests are used in everyday life, and there are many more. Psychological tests are administered in many different settings and sometimes online. They can play a role in determining who becomes a police officer and who doesn't, which parent gets custody of a child, and whether an inmate can be executed. At the pediatrician's office, infants are tested to determine if they are growing and learning at the proper rate for their level of development. The same children, before entering kindergarten, are screened for readiness. As they grow up children take tests in school, and as they approach graduation, many students take the SAT or ACT before applying to college. People of all ages take career interest and personality tests to help them decide what kind of career would best suit them.

Psychological tests are frequently used in the workplace. They inform employers about competencies and personality characteristics of job applicants, helping them make decisions about who should and shouldn't be hired. Psychological tests are also used to assess executives and mid-level managers in order to help them develop their skills and talents, to make decisions about promotions, and to help teams work together. They are also used to determine "fitness for duty" of an employee, for example, after an employee in a public safety position has been arrested for Driving Under the Influence (DUI).

Psychological tests are often used in the legal arena as well, in both civil and criminal cases. Tests might be used to assist in determining the competency of a defendant to stand trial or to plan a rehabilitation program for a juvenile offender. On the civil side, psychological tests help determine culpability and damages in lawsuits related to traumatic brain injury or Posttraumatic Stress Disorder.

Psychological tests also play a role in many basic and applied research studies that inform our daily lives. Does perfectionism contribute to anxiety? Are there sex differences in visual-spatial abilities? What happens after a concussion? Researchers trying to answer these and many other questions rely on psychological tests to choose research subjects and to measure the characteristics they are interested in examining.

WHAT IS A PSYCHOLOGICAL TEST?

Psychological tests are tools used by psychologists, other mental health providers, health care professionals, scientists, educators, administrators, managers, and others tasked with understanding human behavior and making decisions about people. Their purpose is to measure characteristics of human functioning such as personality traits, feelings, attitudes, aptitudes, or abilities. The characteristics are not measured directly; instead, they are inferred from responses to a standardized set of stimuli, that is, a test.

CATEGORIZING PSYCHOLOGICAL TESTS

Tests can be categorized in several different ways, but one of the most basic is whether the test is norm-referenced or criterion-referenced. Norm-referenced tests such as the SAT allow the user to compare the performance of the test taker to that of other individuals or to the test takers' performance on previous administrations of the test. Criterion-referenced tests, such as classroom tests in school, allow the user to determine if the test taker has met a predetermined standard.

Tests are also classified by their functions. Some tests measure abilities, such as verbal or spatial ability. These are characteristics people are thought to be born with. Others measure skills, such as math calculation or driving skills, capacities that are learned or acquired. Other tests measure personality traits, such as conscientiousness, and still others measure symptoms, such as the symptoms of ADHD, depression, or anxiety. Some tests measure complex aspects of human behavior, such as interpersonal and emotional functioning.

Tests can also be classified by how they are administered. Tests of cognitive ability, for example, are often administered individually to the test subject. He or she is asked to solve different kinds of puzzles, some verbal in nature and others perceptual. Many personality tests are *self-report* tests; for these, test subjects answer questions about themselves on their own. The test might ask True/False questions, or it might give the test taker more choices, for example, five possibilities ranging from strongly disagree to strongly agree. The test taker's responses are combined and tabulated into different scales, so that each question makes a small contribution to test results. For some tests, ratings about the test subject are made by others, such as a parent, a spouse, a teacher, or a friend. Projective, or performance-based, tests ask the test taker to respond to specific stimuli, and their responses have few constraints.

All of these kinds of tests have in common the intention to measure one or more aspect of human functioning in a way that produces meaningful results.

THE SCIENCE, HISTORY, AND PRACTICE OF PSYCHOLOGICAL TESTING

The text that follows examines the science, history, and current practice of psychological testing in several domains in which tests are routinely administered. The science of psychological testing is concerned with making sure tests measure what they are supposed to so that results provide accurate data. There are a lot of challenging technical problems in measuring human attributes. As just one example, job applicants want to make a good impression on potential employers and are motivated to *look good* when they take a psychological test as part of the application process. Can a test distinguish between job applicants who are *pretending* to be good candidates and those who are good candidates? How can test developers devise a test that distinguishes between these two types of job candidates? How can they show that the test provides accurate data? These are some of the complicated issues that the science of psychological testing attempts to address.

In the practice realm, those who use psychological tests to make important decisions, such as human resource managers who are responsible for hiring for their organization, must choose tests that have a good base of research support. Only then can they have confidence in test results. They also have to follow laws that are related to the practice of testing, for example, laws that prohibit discrimination and protect privacy, and they also must follow ethical guidelines for their profession.

Practitioners of all sorts, whether they are teachers, managers, therapists, or anyone else who works with people, must also decide if administering a psychological test will help them meet their goals. For example, should a teacher give a test to a student to determine if he or she has mastered the material taught in class? Perhaps a portfolio would be a better means of assessment. Thinking of psychological tests as tools can help practitioners weigh the costs and benefits of administering them.

Exploring the history of psychological testing as it has been applied in specific domains provides a context for understanding how and why practitioners use tests the way that they do. It also allows for a review of the various purposes psychological testing has served over the years and is a reminder that psychological tests are tools that have been used for all kinds of purposes, some of which have been discriminatory or in other ways harmful. It is up to the user to ensure that psychological tests are used to reach worthy goals.

A PERSONAL NOTE

Psychological Testing in Everyday Life attempts to lift a curtain so that readers can understand how psychological tests work as well as the many different functions they serve. My biggest hope for this text is that it encourages readers and those they influence to be thoughtful when they consider what to measure about people, how to measure it, and, equally important, their reasons for measuring it. Psychological tests can be powerful tools and it is vital that they are used for just purposes. Another hope for the text is that it inspires readers to create innovative methods for thinking about and measuring human characteristics. Advances in technology and data analytic techniques should make that possible, and I look forward to seeing what kinds of measurement tools the future brings.

Discussion Questions

1. Consider what you already know about psychological testing and add your own examples of the circumstances in which psychological tests are administered to those described above. Would psychological testing be helpful in other situations as well? Would it be harmful?

2. How would you define psychological testing? Describe assessments or evaluations that are psychological tests and others that are not. How do they differ?

3. What are you curious about when it comes to psychological testing? What do you want to learn?

Research Ideas

1. How are self-report tests written? How do test developers decide how many questions to include, the format for answering them, and how the test is scored? Examine a number of different self-report tests to see the different approaches taken by test authors.

2. What kinds of tests are used by neuropsychologists? What kinds of characteristics do neuropsychologists measure?

3. What is the history of psychological testing in education? How long ago were tests first administered to students, and how have testing practices in education changed since then?

THE SCIENCE OF PSYCHOLOGICAL TESTING

Fundamental Concepts

A psychological test can be devised in a few minutes. Anyone who wants to create a test can quickly come up with questions to answer or tasks to perform and use the responses to measure characteristics or traits of the test takers. For example, if Joseph wants to develop a test to measure emotional sensitivity, he can think about what the concept means and devise questions to evaluate those qualities in the test taker. He might ask, "Do you cry at movies?" and "Do your friends seek you out when they are having problems?" He could invent a scoring system for the responses and create instructions for interpreting results. He could even post the test online so anyone could take it. But how would Joseph know if the test actually measures emotional sensitivity? Would the test be any good at helping people make real-life decisions, such as whether the test taker would make a good partner or employee? Would the test provide reliable information about the test taker to a therapist or school counselor? The information that follows explains what makes a psychological test a good test. It also makes clear why it is essential to use good tests when making decisions or giving professional advice.

The field of psychology devoted to evaluating the quality of psychological tests is *psychometrics*. Psychometrics got its start in the late 19th century when Francis Galton began to measure how humans differ from one another. He came up with important statistical concepts such as the correlation coefficient and the normal distribution. The field has advanced considerably since then, but the basic goal of psychometrics, determining the quality of measurement tools used to assess human attributes or characteristics, hasn't changed.

Human attributes are difficult to measure, in part, because they are hard to define. What would be a good definition for the attributes of anxiety, intelligence, or happiness? These are just a few of a very large number of attributes that psychologists attempt to measure. Psychologists carefully consider how to define the attributes they are interested in measuring. Definitions vary, depending on the point of view of the psychologist and the purpose of measuring the attribute. Before they attempt to measure an attribute, however, psychologists must have its definition in mind because how they define the attribute determines what they measure and how they measure it.

The concept of emotional sensitivity demonstrates this problem. It lacks a clear definition. Does emotional sensitivity mean being aware of emotions in oneself or emotions in others? Does it mean to be quick to respond emotionally to an event or to respond with a lot of intense emotion? Or does it mean to respond emotionally to minor events? It could mean all of these things. The important point is that the attribute of emotional sensitivity must be defined by the psychologist before he or she develops a method of measuring it.

Another challenge in measuring human attributes is that their measurement is imprecise, that is, prone to random error to a far greater degree than measurement in the physical sciences. Random error can be caused by environmental factors, such as when the room a test is administered in is cold and some, but not all, test takers are aggravated or rush to finish because of the temperature. They respond to questions in a way they wouldn't otherwise, and that affects their test scores. Random errors can also be caused by temporary factors related to individual test takers. For example, Joan had to take a personality test for her job, but she was in a bad mood after she had a fight with her boyfriend. She responded to items negatively, reflecting how she felt that day. If she took the test the next day, after she and her boyfriend worked out their problems, she may have answered the same questions differently.

There are other sources of error that are problematic when measuring human attributes or psychological characteristics. Questions about psychological characteristics can be interpreted other than intended or in different ways by different test takers. Also, test takers might use varied frames of reference when answering test questions. This is called reference bias (Duckworth & Yeager, 2015). For example, Annabelle's parents complete rating forms about her behavior for her pediatrician. They answer the exact same questions about the exact same child, such as a question about how much effort Annabelle makes when doing her homework. Her father checks the box for *a little effort,* and her mother checks the box for *a lot of effort.* Both are correct, but they have different reference points for how much effort is a little or a lot when it comes to doing homework. Test developers have to factor in these potential problems and make sure, to the extent possible, that test scores are not impacted by misinterpretations of test questions or reference bias.

Random error is the difference between a person's score on a test and what would be their true score, if that could be determined. Random errors sometimes result in scores that are higher than the true score and sometimes lower, but because they are random they cancel each other out. There are established methods to reduce random error and to estimate the presence of random error in a given test, that is, to determine how consistently and accurately a test measures true scores of test takers. For the proposed emotional sensitivity test, these methods could determine if the test measures emotional sensitivity however it is defined by the researcher in a consistent manner across time and test takers. How close does the test come to providing a true score?

There are other sources of measurement error as well. One troubling source of error, because of its potential impact on groups of individuals, is test bias. Tests may be developed using data from individuals from one culture and used to assess individuals who have a different cultural background (Dana, 2005). The test may not be accurate in predicting the behavior of individuals from other cultures, resulting in test bias.

In addition, test takers can respond to test items inaccurately on purpose, to serve their own agendas. They may *fake good*, purposefully answer items in ways that make them look good, perhaps to an employer, or *fake bad*, purposely answer items that make them look like they have problems, such as when they are trying to falsely claim they have a disability. Socially desirable responding is a common problem that occurs when test takers answer questions in a way that is socially desirable but inaccurate. Test developers have methods of counteracting these kinds of problems. Some tests include validity scales to ferret out whether an individual test taker is responding in an overly positive or negative light. Others are developed with explicit attention to issues of social desirability, ensuring to the extent possible that test items don't lend themselves to socially desirable responding.

A well-constructed psychological test minimizes the impact of random error and the other types of errors that result in inaccurate measurement. Errors are minimized by developing test questions carefully and empirically to reduce the likelihood of misinterpretation and reference bias. Random error is minimized when tests are long, when responses to individual questions measuring the same construct are consistent, and when attributes being measured are carefully defined, have a strong theoretical and empirical foundation, and vary widely among test takers (Miller, Lovler, & McIntire, 2013).

Test developers and end users then use psychometric methods to determine if a test is reliable or consistent enough to use as a measurement tool. The reliability coefficient, described below, is a widely used measure of the extent to which an obtained score is impacted by random error.

Even a very reliable test, one that is only minimally impacted by random or other errors, may not measure the construct (such as emotional sensitivity, intelligence, or depression) it intends to measure. For example, the emotional sensitivity test described above, even if the concept is clearly defined and the test is not overly prone to error, may actually be measuring a characteristic other than emotional sensitivity. Perhaps it measures a different attribute, such as intelligence or pessimism, so that a high score on the test does not reflect emotional sensitivity but instead reflects one of these qualities. Interpreting test results as if they reflected emotional sensitivity in this case would be misleading and would result in the end user making inferences about the test taker that are inaccurate. The aspect of test development concerned with the inferences that can be drawn from a test is called *validity*.

Psychometrics is, in part, the art and science of determining how good a test is at measuring a quality or characteristic consistently every time it is administered (Miller, Lovler, & McIntire, 2013). This definition assumes that nothing else changes, so that the *true score* of a test, the score that is free of random error, remains stable. A test that is developed to minimize random error would get close to the true score of the test taker, the score the test taker would obtain if random error was not a factor. How effective is the test at obtaining a score that is close to the true score for the characteristic being measured? This is called reliability.

Psychometrics is also the art and science of determining how valid the inferences are that are drawn from a test. If a test isn't reliable, if results are not consistent from one administration to the next, and the test doesn't do a good job of establishing a true score, it is not a good measurement tool. It cannot be counted on to provide accurate information about the attribute in question. Thus, establishing the reliability of a test is fundamental to determining the validity of the interpretations of test scores. However, even a test that is reliable can produce results that are not valid for the test's intended purpose.

RELIABILITY

Every test, even one that is very strong from a psychometric perspective, is impacted by random error due to temporary conditions that are not related to the attribute being measured. An obtained score is always a combination of a test taker's true score and random error. Complicating matters, the attributes measured by psychological tests, such as intelligence, memory, or personality traits, are not directly observable. We cannot know, and can never know, true scores for any psychological characteristic; the best we can do is to estimate true scores from obtained scores. If there is too much random error in a test, the obtained scores of test takers will not provide accurate estimates of their true scores.

How do psychologists determine if obtained scores adequately reflect the true scores of test takers, given that their true scores are unknown? Classical test theory, an approach to measuring the reliability of psychological tests, has been used by psychologists to perform this task for more than 80 years (Hambleton & Slater, 1997) and continues to be widely used by test developers. In this model, a psychologist developing a test, or a potential test user, examines the test's *reliability coefficients*, which are essentially correlation coefficients, to determine the test's reliability. (A *correlation* is the extent to which two variables move in relationship with each other. A correlation is high and positive if when one variable goes up, the other goes up to a similar degree. A correlation is low if there is little relationship between how the two variables move, for example, one goes up significantly and the other doesn't move much at all. If one variable goes up and the other goes down to a similar degree, the variables have a strong negative correlation.) A reliability coefficient is a correlation coefficient that measures to what extent scores on two administrations of a test (test-retest reliability), two parts of a test (internal consistency), or parallel versions of a test (alternate forms) are correlated with each other. Adequate reliability depends on the purpose of the test.

Note that reliability coefficients are estimates based on assumptions, such as the assumption that administering a test to the same person twice doesn't change the true score on the test. For this reason, good research on reliability of a test uses a variety of strategies and is done with different groups of test takers, to get the best estimate of the test's reliability.

Cronbach's alpha, based on classical test theory, was first proposed in 1951 (Schweizer, 2011) but remains in widespread use by contemporary test developers. Schweizer (2011) reports that 80% of papers in the *European Journal of Psychological Assessment* in 2010 included Cronbach's alpha coefficient, a measure of internal consistency of a test based on how individual test items correlate with each other.

Item response theory (IRT), an alternative method of establishing reliability, is based on the notion that a response to a test item is related to the test taker's ability (or degree of the attribute under question) and the difficulty of the test item. A mathematical model is applied to predict the response. IRT is used to determine how effective a test is, and how effective individual items are, in measuring a characteristic, considering the predicted response. Embretson (2010) notes that IRT has many advantages over classical test theory and has replaced it in many instances.

What are the problems associated with using a test with low reliability? When comparing results of two tests for a research project, for example, if one test has low reliability there will be a lower correlation with the other test than there would be if the researcher used a more reliable test; therefore, there could be a lack of statistical significance in the findings of the study. For applied purposes, such as employee selection, using a test with low reliability is likely to result in poor decision making.

Getting back to the test on emotional sensitivity, if a test developer actually wanted to create a test and use it to make decisions about people, to understand them better, or to conduct research, she would try to make a reliable test, one in which results were not overly influenced by random error. She would probably make it a lot longer than two questions and would make sure the responses to questions had high correlations with each other. She would study the concept of emotional sensitivity and refine the test to make sure she would be measuring something with a high degree of variability in the population. For this reason, she would choose questions that would be most likely to differentiate people high and low in emotional sensitivity. Once she came up with what seemed to be a good test, she would then measure its reliability.

VALIDITY

The next step in developing a test would be to examine its validity. Unlike the notion of reliability, the question of validity is related to the purpose of the test. Is the emotional sensitivity test valid for setting goals in couple's therapy? Or for selecting peer counselors at a college? Or for choosing a date from a dating website? Validity is also concerned with specific inferences or predictions drawn from test results. What is a valid interpretation of a particular score on a test? Do those who obtain high scores on the emotional sensitivity test make better peer counselors than those who obtain low scores?

Validity is not a property of the test itself; a test is not simply valid or invalid. Instead, examining the validity of a test for a particular purpose informs the test user about the appropriateness of the test for that purpose. Theory, empirical studies, and statistics such as factor analysis all have a place in determining the validity of a test for a given purpose.

Validity remains a controversial topic among psychologists. The *Standards for Educational and Psychological Testing*, a joint venture of three different associations concerned with psychological and educational tests, is the bible for test development and test use, and it was recently revised (APA, 2014). The *Standards* were first published in the 1950s. They have evolved over time, especially on the question of validity and its meaning (Cizek, 2012).

Cizek (2012) notes areas of validity theory in which there is consensus among experts. First, validity applies to inferences made from test scores. Thus, it is necessary to make a statement about the intended inferences, what the test developer expects to be inferred from the scores, to plan validation studies. Second, all validity is construct validity, meaning that all evidence about the validity of test interpretations is related to the construct being measured by the test. Third, validity statements are on a continuum. An inference is valid to a greater or lesser degree, not valid or invalid. Fourth, validation efforts involve the application of values because validity studies are used to justify the use of a test for a particular purpose. Finally, validation is an ongoing endeavor.

Cizek (2012) goes on to note that areas of disagreement among experts, which are not insignificant, include the definition of validity and the boundaries and philosophical underpinnings of the concept. Newton and Shaw (2013) state that the field has been unable to reach agreement over whether the concept of validity ought to embrace the evaluation of measurement aims alone; the evaluation of measurement and decision-making aims; or the evaluation of measurement, decision-making, and broader testing policy aims. (p. 302)

Despite the ongoing controversies, test developers and test users need to determine the validity of test interpretations. Test developers might intend, for example, for high scores on their test to reflect a certain characteristic. Validation studies address the question of whether they in fact do reflect that characteristic. For example, a high score on the Beck Depression Inventory (BDI) is intended to reflect the presence of depression. Validation studies assess whether that is in fact the case. They address the meaning of a test score.

In a validation study of the BDI in a sample of low income African-American medical patients, those who met criteria for major depression on a structured diagnostic interview had higher BDI scores than those who didn't have major depression, supporting the effectiveness of the BDI in assessing depression in low income, African-American medical patients (Grothe et al., 2005). In a different validation study, the Beck Depression Inventory-II (BDI-II) was administered to adolescent psychiatric inpatients along with other measures. Scores on the BDI-II had moderate correlations with scores on measures of *internalizing* disorders (anxiety, depression, low self-esteem), offering evidence for *convergent validity*, and had low correlations with scores on measures of *externalizing* disorders (anger, conduct problems, school problems), offering evidence for *discriminant validity*. Also, BDI-II scores for patients who were clinically diagnosed with major depression were higher than scores for patients diagnosed with conduct disorder. Both sets of findings lend support to the use of the BDI-II in measuring depression in adolescent inpatients (Osman, Kopper, Barrios, Gutierrez, and Bagge, 2004).

There are many more validation studies for the BDI and BDI-II and for a myriad of other psychological tests. How would a validation study for the emotional sensitivity test (let's call it the EST) be conducted? Scores on the EST could be compared with scores on other tests that purport to measure emotional sensitivity or the lack of emotional sensitivity. Experiments could be conducted to determine whether test takers who score high on the EST respond to contrived situations with more emotional sensitivity than those who score low on the scale. Interviews could be undertaken to find out about emotionally sensitive behavior in the test taker's everyday life. Test takers could keep electronic diaries in which they record, or a friend records, his or her emotionally sensitive behaviors throughout the day. There are numerous possibilities.

The concept of validity is also important at the level of the individual because it applies to individual test takers' responses to a test. Did the test taker actually read the questions on the EST, or did he want to get done quickly and simply respond randomly to test items? Was she tired or in a bad mood, causing her to answer in a manner that was inconsistent with her usual thoughts and feelings? Was she motivated to present herself in an overly favorable light, as more or less emotionally sensitive than is in fact the case? Before a psychologist interprets a test score, he must determine that the test taker produced a *valid protocol*. If not, results may not accurately reflect the underlying characteristic that the test is intended to measure, for that administration of the test.

Some tests include *validity scales* as part of the test itself. The MMPI-2, for example, includes scales measuring whether the test taker tried to *look good* or *look bad*, and it includes other scales measuring whether the test taker responded to test items defensively, inconsistently, or randomly. The validity scales are used to determine if scores on the substantive scales, those that measure the characteristics the test is intended to measure, can be meaningfully interpreted for a particular test taker.

In sum, good psychological tests have documented reliability. They are not overly prone to random error. They also have documented validity of the interpretations given to test scores. The test developer might state that he or she believes the test items reflect the characteristics the test intends to measure and that high or low scores on the test can be interpreted in a particular way, but in most real-life circumstances that involve psychological testing, statements made by the test developer will not be sufficient justification for the test user to administer the test, interpret results, and make decisions based on them. Test users need to ensure that the test is reliable, and they need to review results of validation studies that are relevant to how they plan to use the test. Once that is done, the test can be a valuable tool in decision making and problem solving.

Discussion Questions

1. How would you define *happiness* so that it can be measured, and how would you measure it?

2. What is test bias? What are the consequences of test bias for individuals and for society?

3. Discuss how reliability and validity are linked using hypothetical examples.

Research Ideas

1. Choose a specific human attribute, such as frustration tolerance, spatial ability, or trustworthiness, and conduct a literature review to find out how the attribute has been measured by different researchers.

2. Explore how psychological testing has evolved over time. What strategies have researchers used to improve measurement techniques?

3. Investigate new procedures, tools, and technologies used to measure psychological characteristics. What's coming on the market?

4. Examine the controversy among psychologists over the Rorschach Inkblot Method and discuss the current status of the test.

References

American Psychological Association. (2014). *Standards for Educational and Psychological Testing.* Washington, DC: Author.

Cizek, G. J. (2012). Defining and distinguishing validity: Interpretations of score meaning and justifications of test use. *Psychological Methods, 17*(1), 31–43. Retrieved from http://dx.doi .org/10.1037/a0026975

Dana, R. H. (2005). *Multicultural assessment: Principles, applications, and examples.* Mahwah, NJ: Lawrence Erlbaum Associates.

Duckworth, A. L., & Yeager, D. S. (2015). Measurements matter: Assessing personal qualities other than cognitive ability for educational purposes. *Educational Researcher, 44*(4), 237–251.

Embretson, S. E. (Ed). (2010). *Measuring psychological constructs: Advances in model-based approaches.* Washington, DC: American Psychological Association.

Grothe, K. B., Dutton, G. R., Jones, G. N., Bodenlos, J., Ancona, M., & Brantley, P. J. (2005). Validation of the Beck Depression Inventory-II in a low-income African American sample of medical outpatients. *Psychological Assessment, 17*(1), 110–114. doi:10.1037/1040-3590.17.1.110

Hambleton, R. K., & Slater, S. C. (1997). Item response theory models and testing practices: Current international status and future directions. *European Journal of Psychological Assessment, 13*(1), 21–28. doi:10.1027/1015-5759.13.1.21

Miller, L. A., Lovler, R. L., & McIntire, S. A. (2013). *Foundations of psychological testing: A practical approach* (4th ed.). Thousand Oaks, CA: Sage.

Newton, P. E., & Shaw, S. D. (2013). Standards for talking and thinking about validity. *Psychological Methods, 18*(3), 301–319. doi:10.1037/a0032969

Osman, A., Kopper, B. A., Barrios, F., Gutierrez, P. M., & Bagge, C. L. (2004). Reliability and validity of the Beck Depression Inventory–II with adolescent psychiatric inpatients. *Psychological Assessment, 16*(2), 120–132. doi:10.1037/1040-3590.16.2.120

Schweizer, K. (2011). On the changing role of Cronbach's α in the evaluation of the quality of a measure. *European Journal of Psychological Assessment, 27*(3), 143–144. doi:10.1027/1015-5759/ a000069

3

PSYCHOLOGICAL TESTING IN EDUCATION

Comparing Student Outcomes Across Nations With the PISA and the TIMSS

LEARNING OBJECTIVES

- Describe several uses of psychological tests in education

- Compare and contrast the PISA and the TIMSS

- Discuss the role of values and goals when choosing tests to administer for educational purposes

- Contrast the test development process for the PISA and TIMSS

- Decide which test, the PISA or TIMSS, is a better test and defend your decision

- Discuss how an understanding of test goals contributes to the interpretation of test data

Stan, a 15 year-old boy from Oklahoma, sat down in the front of the classroom, facing a computer screen. He was about to take a math test. His teacher told the class that test results would not affect their grades, so Stan was feeling more relaxed than he usually felt before a test. His teacher also advised the students to do as well as they could on the test. Their scores would be put together with scores of other students to reflect how well 15-year-olds understood math concepts. Scores for the district, state, and country would be tabulated and results compared to those of 15-year-olds throughout the world. Stan was ready to get to work.

Several months later, staff from the National Center for Education Statistics (NCES) in Washington, DC, had their first look at the results. The news was mixed. Students from the United States scored below students from several other countries as they had in years past, but they hadn't fallen further behind. NCES staff planned to analyze the results, inform the public about them, and make recommendations about improving math instruction.

PSYCHOLOGICAL TESTS IN EDUCATION

Psychological tests are administered in educational settings to meet a wide range of goals. By the time they are in college, students have taken hundreds of tests. In individual school districts across the United States, classroom teachers create tests to find out if students are making progress in math, reading, or social studies; the school principal administers standardized tests to an entire grade to get an estimate of each student's ability and an overall sense of student needs; the superintendent of the district makes sure standardized tests of academic progress are administered as required by the state board of education; and the school psychologist administers tests to determine if a child who is struggling to learn qualifies for special education services. High school students take standardized tests such as the SAT to submit as part of their application to college, and college graduates take the GRE or other standardized tests when they apply to graduate school.

The administration of standardized, grade-level tests in core subjects such as math or language arts is widespread but controversial. Some parents opt out of standardized testing for their children because they disagree with the goals of testing, believe that the tests are too hard or don't track the curriculum, disagree with the use of test results to evaluate teachers, or for other reasons.

Standardized tests are employed on an even broader scale, to measure the effectiveness of countries in educating their students and to compare the educational programs of countries or regions to one another, rank ordering them. These tests influence national and international education policies at the highest levels.

For this chapter, we are going to review two not very widely known psychological tests used in education, the test that Stan took, the Programme for International Student Assessment, or PISA, and another one that serves a similar purpose, the Trends in International Mathematics and Science Study, or TIMSS. These tests have an impact on education systems in entire countries, far beyond school districts and states, but they are administered to comparatively few students.

INTERNATIONAL COMPARISONS OF EDUCATIONAL ACHIEVEMENT: HISTORY AND GOALS

The International Association for the Evaluation of Educational Achievement (IEA), the organization responsible for the TIMSS, originated in the 1950s under UNESCO, an arm of the United Nations. Scholars in education and sociology, along with psychometricians, wanted to compare the results of education across different educational systems to understand and improve educational outcomes, and they wanted to rely on data to make the comparisons. In order to achieve their goals, a test was developed to administer to students in different countries. The first study was conducted in 1960, and it measured achievement in math, reading, geography, science, and nonverbal abilities in 11 European countries, Israel, and the United States.

Measurement of educational outcomes across countries for different subject matter including reading, math, science, technology, civics, and recently, financial literacy, has grown in importance since then. More countries (and other *educational systems*, such as states) participate each year, and the IEA has gained a competitor in data collection, a testing program developed by the Organisation for Economic Co-operation and Development (OECD), as discussed below. Contemporary methods of quantitative data analysis are likely to make the measurement of educational outcomes across countries easier, more thorough, and more accurate.

In addition to comparing educational outcomes across nations with a focus on excellence in education, another goal of measuring educational outcomes is to improve equity, or fairness, in educational outcomes within an educational system. For example, the PISA measures educational outcomes for immigrant and nonimmigrant students with the goal of finding out which countries are most successful in improving educational outcomes for immigrant students. Educational researchers can investigate how the more successful countries succeed in meeting that goal, and other countries can improve their own educational practices to meet similar goals. Similarly, TIMSS data are used to work toward minimizing the achievement gap between high and low achieving students.

PISA researchers use the concept of resilience to further an understanding of how to promote equity in education. Resilient students are those who are socioeconomically disadvantaged but exceed expectations for educational outcomes. PISA results suggest that educational policy can help individual students who are disadvantaged become resilient. Some countries, such as Singapore and Vietnam, are more successful at achieving this outcome than others.

INTERNATIONAL TESTS OF ACADEMIC SKILLS: THE PISA AND THE TIMSS

The PISA and TIMSS measure different kinds of academic skills in the same subject areas. Although they seem to be measuring the same capacities, such as how well a student solves math problems, they are in fact measuring different phenomena. To put it simply, the PISA measures how well a student applies math skills to solve real-world problems, and the TIMSS measures what math students have learned and how skillful they are at math calculation. Students who were never taught applied problem-solving approaches to math are not likely to perform as well on a test of mathematical problem-solving as students who were taught to apply mathematical solutions to problems. Does that mean they are not as good at math? It might, if being good at math is defined as being good at mathematical problem-solving. It might not, if being good at math is defined as something else, such as being skillful in mathematical calculation. Choosing to administer one test or the other could result in very different conclusions about how accomplished students are in math. The choice of one test or another makes a difference to the outcome of testing and reflects the underlying values and goals of decision makers. Although two tests may appear to be measuring the same thing at first glance, a closer look may reveal they are not. An examination of the PISA and the TIMSS makes this clear.

It also makes plain that psychological test results can have an impact at the highest levels as well as on the life of an individual test taker. For example, most people have to pass a written driving test prior to getting a driver's license; test results in this instance have a major influence on the life of the test taker. The PISA and TIMSS are different. Results of both of these tests have little impact on individual test takers, but they may have a significant impact on educational policies and practices across entire nations.

The PISA

To reach its goal of measuring the effectiveness of a country's educational system, the PISA is administered to a carefully selected sample of 15-year-old students in each participating country. Scores are calculated and countries ranked on the basis of student scores. The test was administered for the first time in 2000, and it is administered again every three years. In the United States, 42 students from each of 240 public and private schools took the test in 2015. Seventy-two educational systems (nations and some states) across the globe participated.

When the results of the PISA are released, they are reviewed by government representatives and educational organizations and reported by the press. The Alliance for Excellent Education (AEE), a nonprofit aimed at reforming high schools and advocating at the federal level for at-risk students, denotes a day soon after the results are released as *Pisa Day*. Pisa Day explores the implications of the results in a day-long digital event available to anyone who is interested. The event has its own website: www.pisaday.org. PISA Day 2016 included webinars on the use of PISA results in developing education policy, evaluating the economic impact of education, and improving education in schools and across districts.

The PISA measures the capacity of 15-year-olds to apply their knowledge in reading, math, and science to real-life situations. The United States has not done as well as most Americans would like on PISA. The NCES reports that on the 2015 test in math, the United States ranked 36 of the 69 education systems (nces.ed.gov) that took the test. Rankings were a bit higher for reading and science but still below that of many countries, from Estonia to Japan. Another worrisome trend for the United States is that PISA math scores decreased from 2012 to 2015.

PISA was created by the OECD, an international organization that collects and analyzes data on a broad range of topics including health, agriculture, economics, and education. The stated goal of PISA is to determine how well 15-year-olds in participating countries are prepared to meet the challenges they are likely to encounter in the future. A carefully selected representative sample of students from each participating country is administered a two-hour exam that includes multiple choice and open response questions based on situations that students might face in real life. The tests are scored and results for each student are categorized by level of proficiency. Overall results are tabulated and countries are ranked in math, science, and reading on the basis of average student scores, and rankings are interpreted as a reflection of the educational system within each country.

The PISA answers all kinds of other questions too. For example, results from the most recent test indicate that 20% of students across all OECD countries are not proficient in reading, while, in a few countries, 25% of students have high levels of proficiency in math. They also indicate that some countries do better than others in providing equitable educational outcomes for all students, regardless of their backgrounds.

Questions on the PISA ask students to apply knowledge in math and science to real world situations, that is, they ask students to solve real-world problems. The items are in groups of questions about a single topic such as car speed and distance, the average height of a group of girls, or what happens to runners in hot weather. Each item includes multiple choice, True/False, and open-ended questions. The items are too complex to include here but sample questions are readily available on the OECD website (OECD.org).

From the development of the test to the interpretation of results, the PISA is a complex product. PISA administrators have to choose a representative sample of students from each country as well as develop and translate test questions that are free of cultural bias. They have to decide what the test should measure, how it should be scored, and how test results should be described. Those who arranged for the test to be developed and administered are responsible for making sense of the findings and for using the findings to inform educational decisions.

The TIMSS

The TIMSS is a product of IEA, a nonprofit international organization begun in the late 1950s for the purpose of comparing educational systems in order to learn about effective educational practices around the world. The IEA first administered tests internationally in 1960. The TIMSS was administered for the first time in 1995, and it has been administered every four years since then, most recently in 2015. The test is given to 4th and 8th graders in more than 50 countries, including the United States. Schools in which the TIMSS is administered are selected randomly, as are the children within the schools. Results are reported for the country as a whole and are compared with results from other countries. Some individual schools and districts also use the TIMSS to inform their curriculum, after it is administered for its primary purpose, which is to compare the effectiveness of education in math and science in different countries.

The TIMSS is developed at Boston College by content and measurement experts and education professionals. Content and cognitive domains included in each test are carefully chosen. The 4th grade content domains that are measured include number, geometric shapes, and data display. Algebra is added for the 8th grade test. Knowing, applying, and reasoning are the cognitive domains for both grades. The cognitive domains are the behaviors students need to apply to the content in order to answer the test questions.

Guidelines for writing test questions are both general and very specific, and include, for example, instructions for how to write multiple choice questions and general instructions for avoiding bias. Items are developed in committees, piloted, and tested.

Sample TIMSS questions are straightforward and include, for 8th grade, problems about the sum of interior angles of a pentagon, dividing fractions, and how the number 36 can be expressed as a product of prime factors.

Like the PISA, the TIMSS is a complex product. Test developers and administrators make many important decisions that impact test results and their interpretation. They decide on a method for selecting representative samples of students to take the test, ensure questions are translated properly and are free of cultural bias, choose the content and wording of test questions, and create a scoring system and method of interpreting test results. As with the PISA, when results are in, consumers of test data, which include policy makers and educational administrators at the highest levels, use them to improve educational outcomes for millions of students in the United States and other countries.

PISA VERSUS TIMSS

Both the PISA and TIMSS seek to answer questions about the effectiveness of education in mathematics and other subjects in different educational systems. How is the United States doing relative to other nations in math instruction? Which educational systems have the most effective programs in math instruction? Have educational outcomes improved in Canada? How about in South Korea? These are the kinds of questions both tests attempt to answer.

Looking at the data for the United States, however, the PISA and TIMSS provide different answers to the same questions. The same is true when reviewing the results for many other countries. For example, for 4th graders in 2015, the United States scored higher than 34 other educational systems (these are mostly other countries but include some states) and lower than 10 on the TIMSS. For 8th graders in 2015, the United States scored higher than 24 educational systems and lower than eight. East Asian countries scored at the highest levels on the TIMSS for both 4th and 8th grades. Thus, on the TIMSS, the United States did better than most other educational systems, although it was not the highest performing educational system; however, the United States did not do as well on the most recent administration of the PISA. The United States scored at about the middle relative to other educational systems in science and reading and below the middle in math. Singapore, Estonia, China, Finland, Japan, and Canada are some of the countries that did better than the United States on the PISA.

Why the difference in outcome? Is it because the students who were tested were different ages, about 9 and 13 for the TIMSS and 15 for the PISA? Were students sampled differently, coming from different districts? Were there mistakes made in test development, so that one test is better than the other? The educational systems to which the United States is compared are not exactly the same for the two tests. Does that make a difference?

It is likely that none of these issues contributed to the different outcomes of the two tests. The discrepant results are more likely due to the different philosophies underlying mathematics education on which the two tests are based, and the exposure of students to that philosophy of mathematics education in the classroom. The TIMSS is curriculum based and a test of formal mathematical knowledge, while the PISA is based on the application of mathematical knowledge, gained in and out of school, to real-world situations. Students who do well on the PISA tend to be educated in countries that employ a math curriculum based on Real Mathematics Education (RME), a philosophy of mathematics education that takes a problem-solving approach to teaching math (www.brookings.edu/research/international-tests-are-not-all-the-same), while the TIMSS is based on a more traditional mathematics curriculum.

Both tests are rigorously developed by content and measurement experts. They have strong psychometrics and use valid techniques to representatively sample student populations. They both effectively measure math skills, but they measure different kinds of math skills. The PISA has more open-ended questions that require students to examine data and make connections, while the TIMSS has more multiple choice questions that require students to solve factual problems. The PISA and TIMSS have different goals. The PISA aims to find out how well students are prepared to use math in adult life, while the TIMSS aims to find out how much math students have learned at different points in their formal education.

Which is a better test of a nation's effectiveness in math education? It depends. Math education is a controversial topic and has gone back and forth in approach and emphasis over the years. For those who believe a problem-oriented approach to math education is best, the PISA will be a better test, but for those who support a more traditional, formal mathematics education curriculum, the TIMSS will be best. The question, which is a better test, exposes deeper concerns and disagreements about the purpose and goals of education as a whole. What do students need to be successful individually and to support the growth of a nation?

As is evident in comparing the results of these two tests, very careful attention to the purpose of a test and the values and philosophies underlying it are just as important as careful attention to test construction. They go hand in hand.

STAN'S EXPERIENCE WITH THE PISA

Stan, the 15-year-old student at the beginning of the chapter, took the PISA. He never found out how he did, nor did any of his classroom teachers. That was OK with Stan. He had forgotten about the test altogether. By the time PISA results were made available so that policy makers could learn from them, Stan was close to high school graduation and taking precalculus to get ready for college. He had a lot of other things on his mind.

Although Stan didn't know it, school administrators were considering changes in the math curriculum that would promote a problem-solving approach to learning math, a goal at the state level. State education officials wanted students to do better on the PISA the next time it was administered. By the time a new math curriculum was ready for use in the classroom, Stan was in college and his little brother, Isaac, was in middle school. Stan learned about the new math curriculum from his parents. They were struggling to help Isaac with his homework.

CONCLUSION

The PISA and the TIMSS are very large-scale testing programs that have a common purpose: to compare educational outcomes across different educational systems, primarily across different countries around the world. Results of both tests are used by educational policy makers and researchers in the United States and elsewhere to improve educational outcomes, focusing on both excellence and equity.

The PISA and TIMSS measure educational outcomes differently. For math, the example discussed above, the PISA measures applied problem-solving skills gained anywhere, while the TIMSS measures the mastery of math skills and knowledge learned in the classroom. As might be expected, results of the two tests are not the same. The choice of one test or another makes a difference to the outcome of testing, not only for math achievement but when measuring all kinds of psychological phenomena.

A comparison of the two tests also makes clear the importance of values and goals in testing. They are always present, no matter how straightforward the purpose of testing seems to be. Testing for achievement in math is a good example because it seems like it would be value free. As shown above, it isn't. Those who make decisions about the need for testing must pay attention to why they want to measure something. What is important about it? That will help them set goals for their testing program and to choose tests wisely to meet them.

Discussion Questions

1. If you were a journalist reporting on the results of the PISA and TIMSS, what kinds of information would you provide to your readers, and why?

2. If you were given the task of creating a test to administer for a school district, what kinds of questions would you ask of the leaders in the district? What would you need to know to make a good choice?

3. How would the values and goals of policy makers and school leaders impact test results in areas of education other than math?

Research Ideas

1. Review the literature on test development for tests at the high school level, choosing one subject area. How are standardized tests developed as compared to classroom tests? Focus on both the form of the test and the content, and consider how values impact the process of test development.

2. Review and discuss PISA or TIMSS related research. What topics are of interest to researchers? How does research contribute to improving the test?

3. How would you measure educational outcomes in areas not covered by the PISA or TIMSS, such as civic responsibility, literature, creativity, or music appreciation? Review the literature to find out how experts measure educational outcomes in an area of interest to you. Discuss the effectiveness of measurement tools, how they were developed, and how they can be improved.

PSYCHOLOGICAL TESTING IN APPLIED RESEARCH

LEARNING OBJECTIVES

- Describe the various functions that psychological tests serve in psychological research
- Identify the steps that researchers took when they developed the Multidimensional Assessment of Preschool Disruptive Behavior (MAP-DB)
- Discuss when it is acceptable to use a very brief psychological test when conducting research
- Discuss the importance of carefully defining the construct that will be studied prior to devising methods of measuring it
- Name the factors researchers consider when they decide if a measure is appropriate to use in an experiment

Jason, a sophomore at a large public university, signed on to be a research subject for a psychology experiment. He saw a sign posted on his dormitory bulletin board offering students $50.00 to participate, and he needed the money. He would have to complete questionnaires a few times over the next two semesters, fill out a diary about his caffeine intake for a month, and go to a lab in the psychology department to take some tests that had to do with attention. The research was about the effects of caffeine on attention, but he didn't know any more about it than that.

Dr. Jenkins was the researcher responsible for the experiment. She was studying the placebo effect for caffeine as part of a larger study about the effects of caffeine on attention. To conduct the experiment, Dr. Jenkins needed to find a good way to measure how much caffeine test subjects consumed on a regular basis because test subjects who had too much tolerance to the effects of caffeine would have to be excluded. She also wanted to exclude other subjects from her experiment, those whose personality traits made them especially vulnerable to placebo effects. She had already completed other research on attention, and she knew how to measure attention in the lab. She also knew which personality test she would use in her experiment to measure vulnerability to placebo effects. She had to do a literature review, however, to find a good way to measure caffeine consumption. She discovered the Caffeine Consumption Questionnaire–Revised (Irons, Bassett, Prendergast, Landrum, & Heinz, 2016), and after reviewing the psychometrics behind it, she decided to use that test along with a caffeine consumption diary. She felt that this would ensure better accuracy in measuring average caffeine consumption than either approach alone.

APPLIED PSYCHOLOGICAL RESEARCH: HISTORY AND GOALS

Experiments in psychology were conducted as early as the late 1800s, and applied research using psychological tests was conducted soon after. For example, in 1920, in an effort to understand why previous research had resulted in low correlations between intelligence test results and grades, researchers examined the correlation between intelligence test results and grades of students in high schools as compared to military academies. The correlation between intelligence test scores and grades was higher for military academies than for high schools, leading the authors to suggest that methods of instruction in the military academies had students working at "maximum efficiency" (Burtt & Arps, 1920, p. 293).

Psychologists conduct basic and applied research to further their understanding of all kinds of psychological phenomena. Without psychological experiments and the tests they rely on, we wouldn't know whether online cognitive behavior therapy can help with procrastination (Rozental, Forsell, Svensson, Andersson, & Carlbring, 2015) or why lonely teenagers stay lonely (Vanhalst, Soenens, Luyckx, Van Petegem, Weeks, & Asher, 2015). These are just two examples of many. Applied research aims to solve problems, while basic research aims to improve the understanding of underlying psychological mechanisms. Applied research might focus, for example, on how to improve memory functioning in older adults, while basic research might focus on memory functioning in pigeons to understand more about learning and memory under stress or with higher or lower rates of reinforcement.

In both basic and applied psychological research, and in other kinds of research involving human subjects, psychological tests are used to measure a very wide variety of psychological functions and characteristics including cognitive abilities, memory functioning, academic skills, personality traits, symptoms of mental disorders, and many other psychological constructs both narrow and broad. Researchers must choose the tests they use in experiments with a lot of care. If a researcher uses a psychological test that does not accurately measure the construct in question, the results of their experiment will be irrelevant and the research wasteful. Even worse, the results of an experiment relying on ineffective measurement tools can be misleading.

In a typical psychological experiment, researchers test hypotheses by varying an independent variable, such as caffeine intake, and examining the effect on one or more dependent variables, for example, attention to a task. An example of a hypothesis might be that caffeine improves attention to a task in individuals who have Attention Deficit Hyperactivity Disorder (ADHD). A more complex hypothesis might be that caffeine improves attention for people who have ADHD more than it improves attention for people who don't have ADHD, or that caffeine improves attention for people who have ADHD but not as much as stimulant medication improves attention for people who have ADHD. The hypothesis could be based on theory or on the results of earlier research, or both, and the results of the experiment may have clinical implications or relevance to an understanding of more fundamental processes, such as the underlying causes of ADHD.

Psychological tests can be used to select subjects for the experiment (people who have ADHD and people who don't have ADHD) and to measure dependent variables (attention to a task). They can also be used to measure confounding variables, such as personality traits. Confounding variables are those that affect the dependent variable aside from the variable that is purposely manipulated for the experiment, in this example, caffeine intake. An example of a confounding variable for the caffeine study might be the personality trait of conscientiousness as conscientiousness could increase attentiveness to a task regardless of caffeine intake, *confounding* the results of the study.

It should be evident from the example above that the psychometric qualities of tests used in research can have a significant impact on results of an experiment. If the test employed by a researcher to determine if research subjects have ADHD doesn't accurately distinguish between people who have ADHD and those who don't, subjects will not be selected in a meaningful way. If a test for attention to a task is actually measuring something else, such as intelligence, it might not reflect the impact of fluctuations in caffeine intake, the independent variable. If a personality measure does not accurately identify subjects who have high degrees of conscientiousness, the confounding variable of conscientiousness will not be properly evaluated.

To demonstrate some of the ways that psychological tests are used in psychology experiments, this chapter focuses on research in three areas: early childhood tantrums, homesickness, and what makes people happy. These areas of research all have relevance to everyday life. All children have tantrums when they are young, most people experience homesickness at some point in their lives, and everyone wants to be happy. The research on temper tantrums demonstrates how a psychological test about a complex subject can be thoughtfully developed in order to answer research questions. Research on homesickness is much more problematic. As will be seen, measures of homesickness are limited, so much so that a research review (Stroebe, Schut, & Nauta, 2015) included studies that measured homesickness with just one question. Conclusions that can be drawn from over 50 studies on homesickness are tentative and not very far reaching. Research on happiness is part of the growing field of positive psychology. Even though happiness is a vague, hard-to-define concept, researchers have devised methods of measuring happiness that are good enough that the research can be replicated; that is, it can be repeated in a different laboratory with the same results.

THE MAP-DB, A TOOL TO MEASURE TEMPER TANTRUMS

All children have tantrums from time to time. How would one go about measuring temper tantrums, and why would anyone want to? A group of researchers has been studying whether preschoolers' tantrums are a part of normal development or an indication of development that has gone awry, and they created a test to answer this question (Wakschlag et al., 2014). The test can help researchers understand the development of psychopathology and identify its early markers, and it may even help clinicians prevent the development of psychopathology in individual children.

The test that Wakschlag and colleagues created is called the Multidimensional Assessment of Preschool Disruptive Behavior (MAP-DB) (Wakschlag et al., 2012; Wakschlag et al., 2014). Researchers used the MAP-DB to document a range of temper tantrums from normal to problematic. In a later study, they created a framework that provides a model of problem behaviors in preschoolers. The research is aimed at answering questions, such as how do we know where a child's behaviors lie on a spectrum from normal to abnormal, and when should a parent be concerned about the frequency and severity of a young child's tantrum behavior, or in other words, when is tantrum behavior beyond the normal range? The research also addresses more theoretical concerns, such as how to understand temper loss in the context of development.

The MAP-DB (Wakschlag et al., 2010) was developed by a team. Members of the team were experts in different areas including normal development, disruptive behavior, and early childhood clinical assessment. The team clarified the constructs they were exploring, generated items, reviewed the items to see how well they captured the constructs, examined the wording and ease of understanding the items, and decided which items would be maintained and which would be discarded. The final item pool for the initial test included 111 items. The researchers asked parents to rate the items in terms of frequency of occurrence over the previous month on a scale of zero to five. Focus groups were employed to determine the terms commonly used by the test subjects to ensure questions would be worded appropriately. Items covered tantrum behavior, aggression, noncompliance, and low concern for others, as well as triggers for the behavior and the context the behavior occurred in. Of the original 111 items, 78 were retained following a data reduction and modeling process.

In one study of the MAP-DB (Wakschlag et al., 2012), researchers hypothesized that some of the items reflected normal misbehavior, while other items reflected problem behavior. Results of the research, conducted with close to 1,500 parents who filled out the MAP-DB and other questionnaires, indicated that most preschoolers exhibited tantrums within the month, but fewer than 10% of preschoolers had tantrums every day. Thus, if a preschooler had a tantrum every day, his or her behavior was atypical. Results also indicated that there were some items on the MAP-DB that did not have to occur frequently to suggest a high likelihood of problem behavior. Overall, the researchers concluded from the data that daily tantrums, tantrums that last more than five minutes, or atypical tantrum behaviors, such as tantrums accompanied by aggression, tantrums occurring in the presence of adults other than parents, or tantrums that occur abruptly for no apparent reason are "developmentally meaningful indicators of concern" (Wakschlag et al., 2012, p. 8).

In a later study using the MAP-DB, Wakschlag et al. (2014) found that four dimensions (Temper Loss, Aggression, Noncompliance, and Low Concern for Others) fit the data very well, indicating that these dimensions, in combination, explain early childhood disruptive behavior. With a closer examination of the data, they were able to determine that some items are at a level indicating severe problems when they occur every day, while other items reflect severe behavior problems when they occur less often. Behaviors on the Aggression and Low Concern for Others dimensions did not have to occur as frequently as behaviors on the Temper Loss and Noncompliance dimensions to indicate the likelihood of severe behavior problems. Aggression items include, for example, threatening and getting into fights. Low Concern for Others items include not seeming to care about a parent's feelings and continuing to do something that scared or upset someone.

Thus, the researchers showed that it is possible to distinguish between normal misbehavior and abnormal behavior in early childhood. Normal misbehavior occurs in expected contexts and is more flexible and less extreme than behavior that might be an indicator of future behavior or mood problems. However, if misbehavior occurs very frequently, for example, if a child has a tantrum every day, his or her behavior is in the abnormal range. Other abnormal behaviors in early childhood are those that are intense, inflexible, provocative, and occur in unexpected contexts, such as with adults other than parents. Even if these kinds of behaviors occur infrequently, they are unusual for young children and may indicate the presence of problems that need to be addressed.

Although the data have not yet been clinically validated, in other words, shown to be consistent with other data that is clinically meaningful, the research has implications for screening in early childhood. It answers the question of when parents or others should be concerned about a young child's misbehavior.

HOMESICKNESS RESEARCH

Homesickness is a normal but distressing feeling that children, teenagers, and adults sometimes experience when away from home. It usually diminishes over time, and it goes away altogether when the affected person returns home, the quickest and easiest treatment. However, like early childhood problem behavior, homesickness exists on a continuum. At the severe end of the continuum, homesickness can result in extreme levels of distress and problems such as dropping out of school or leaving a job.

Research on homesickness can be clinically useful; it can contribute to treating severe homesickness in those individuals who are in significant distress. It can also be used to develop prevention programs for situations that commonly result in homesickness, such as attending summer overnight camp, going away to college, or moving away from home for a job or military service. In addition, understanding the causes, prevalence, and trajectory of homesickness can help explain aspects of healthy development, including attachment to home, the use of coping skills, and resilience in the face of adversity.

Homesickness seems like it should be easy to define as most people are familiar with the experience and know what it feels like to be homesick. When conducting research, however, the details are significant. Homesickness has been defined by researchers as "a negative emotional state primarily due to separation from home and attachment persons, characterized by longing for and preoccupation with home, and often with difficulties adjusting to the new place" (Stroebe, Schut, & Nauta, 2015) and as "the distress or impairment caused by an actual or anticipated separation from home. It is characterized by preoccupying thoughts of home and attachment objects" (Thurber, 1995). These are just two examples. Note the subtle differences in the two definitions. Does homesickness cause distress (a negative emotional state), or does it cause behavior problems (impairment), or does it cause both? Does it cause difficulties in adjustment? Do homesick individuals long for the people they are attached to or home itself?

Thurber and Sigman (1998), in one example of a measure of homesickness, created the Rate Your Day-Revised (RYD-R), a 15-item rating scale developed for research on a homesickness prevention program conducted at a summer camp. On the RYD-R, at the end of a day at camp, research subjects rate each of the 15 items on a scale from 1 to 10, 1 meaning *not at all* to 10 meaning *very much*. Examples include, "I felt WORRIED, I felt RELAXED, and I felt SAD." Three items on the RYD-R are specific to homesickness, and scores on the three items are added together for a homesickness scale. The homesickness scale was validated as a measure of homesickness by comparing results of the RYD-R to results of clinical interviews, observer ratings, and "standardized self-reports of negative emotion" (Thurber & Sigman, 1998, p. 917). The RYD-R was successfully used in a study (Thurber, 2005) that examined the effect of a prevention program on homesickness at a summer overnight camp. The study concluded that the prevention program the author employed was successful in reducing homesickness.

Stroebe et al. (2015) reviewed more than 50 journal articles that reported research on homesickness. They included studies that relied on single-item homesickness measures as well as those that relied on more complex measures of homesickness (HS), stating that "given the paucity of information with psychometrically valid scales particularly among children, it was deemed better to retain these studies (particularly because a single question about HS is likely to be quite valid)" (p. 3).

Based on their review, Stroebe et al. (2015) attempted to draw conclusions about a number of issues related to homesickness. They examined the prevalence of homesickness but found that different ways of measuring homesickness led to different prevalence estimates, as did examining different away-from-home experiences, such as going away to college or relocating for a job. They also examined the consequences of homesickness. According to the studies they reviewed, these include distress, mental and physical health problems, and rumination. However, due to measurement challenges, it was difficult to sort out from the research which came first. For example, does rumination cause homesickness or does homesickness cause rumination? Various studies they reviewed also sought to understand who gets homesick, what makes someone vulnerable to the most severe forms of homesickness, and what causes homesickness.

The authors note that they could only draw tentative conclusions about these questions, despite reviewing over 50 studies, due to limitations of the research and the variability in definitions of homesickness and the populations that were studied. Stroebe et al. (2015) concluded their review with a multitude of additional questions that research on homesickness could address:

> How early in life can one become homesick? How does one become so strongly attached to one's home, as well as those who live there, that one suffers extreme HS on leaving? What is the role of parental behavior in separation situations? Can HS be considered chronic and if so, under what circumstances? Can it be "cured"? Is professional intervention adequate? (p. 12)

HAPPINESS

Research on happiness is part of the growing field of positive psychology, where happiness is often equated with the concept of subjective well-being. There is a tremendous amount of research in this area. Here, we will consider one specific study with a finding robust enough that it was one of the minority of studies that were successfully replicated in the University of Virginia's Reproducibility Project (Open Science Collaboration, 2015). Larsen and McKibban (2008) conducted the original study with undergraduates in the United States and Seibel and colleagues (Seibel et al., 2015) replicated the study with Dutch undergraduate students, using Dutch versions of the self-report tests that Larsen and McKibban used in the original study.

Is happiness associated with having what one wants, wanting what one has, neither, or both? The researchers found that people who have what they want, to a greater extent than other people, are happier than other people, regardless of how much they have or to what extent they want what they have. This would suggest that pursuing and obtaining what one wants contributes to happiness, whether it's something small or large. Being happy with what one has is a different matter, one that research also finds contributes to overall happiness. The researchers looked at material items as well as skills, accomplishments, and relationships. Happiness was associated with getting what one wants and wanting what one has in all of these areas, except for relationships, where having more relationships is more important to happiness than wanting the ones already in place.

The researchers established their findings using a brief and seemingly simple psychological test, the Satisfaction With Life Scale (SWLS) (Diener, Emmons, Larsen, & Griffin, 1985). To develop the scale, Diener et al. began with 48 questions that had to do with life satisfaction. After factor analysis, items related to mood were eliminated. Of those that were left, similar items were dropped, leaving a scale that contained just five questions. The scale was found to have good reliability and to correlate well with other measures of life satisfaction and related personality traits. The SWLS has been extensively researched, is widely used, and has been translated into many languages. It was successfully used in the research on happiness described above, in both the initial study and in its replication.

Researchers were able to conclude from their study on happiness that having what one wants contributes to happiness, with the implication that having realistic *wants* and pursuing them successfully is a good way to increase feelings of happiness. Wanting what one already has also contributes to feelings of happiness, implying that appreciating what one has is another good way to increase feelings of happiness. *Wants* in this happiness study include accomplishments, relationships, and skills, as well as material possessions.

JASON'S EXPERIENCE AS A RESEARCH SUBJECT

Jason, the college student who participated in Dr. Jenkins's experiment, completed his part of the research project and earned his $50.00. Although he didn't know it, his data was included in the study because he was neither a heavy caffeine user nor especially suggestible to placebo effects. For the personality test, he had to answer a lot of questions, choosing between True and False. That was a little difficult as the answer was often in the middle. The research assistant who gave him the test told him to choose the answer that was closest to accurate for him, and he did. He found the attention test more interesting; it seemed like a computer game. He had to click on a button when he saw items of the same color and size, but he was not to click on it when the items were different in either color or size. First, though, he had to drink something that seemed like an energy drink. He found out after the attention test that the energy drink didn't contain caffeine or anything else to keep him awake. He was told to come to the lab before having any coffee for the day, so when he found out there was no caffeine in the drink, his next stop was the cafeteria to get a cup of coffee. He knew he couldn't focus in his psychology class without it.

As for Dr. Jenkins, she was able to complete her study after excluding data from quite a few subjects. There were a lot of serious coffee drinkers among the students, and there were a few students who were quite suggestible. With funding from her research grant, she was able to collect enough data to finish the project. As she hypothesized based on her literature search, she was able to show a small but statistically significant placebo effect for caffeine, although the subjects who actually had caffeine in their energy drink did better on the attention task than the placebo group. She was thinking about the next step in her project, to enhance the effectiveness of the placebo by having subjects think the energy drink, in reality a placebo, was exceptionally good at improving attention. She was pretty sure it would work, but first, she needed the project to pass the institutional review board. The project involved deception, so she wasn't sure if she would succeed.

CONCLUSION

There are thousands of psychological tests in the American Psychological Association (APA) compendium of tests (see PsycTests at www.apa.org/pubs/databases/psyctests/index.aspx), many developed by researchers specifically for a research study or group of studies. As shown above, designing tests to measure specific facets of human behavior can be a complex but successful undertaking, as evident in the research on tantrum behavior. Tests can also be very simple and still be reliable and valid for their intended purpose, even if the goal of the test is to measure a hard to define concept such as happiness. A test of life satisfaction came down to five items after careful analysis, and findings based on test results were robust enough that they were reproduced in a different culture by a different research team. In contrast, the research on homesickness has not led to clear-cut findings, even though it is a much narrower topic than happiness and one that is familiar to most people from personal experience. Homesickness has been defined in various ways by different researchers, and researchers also use different measures of homesickness. Sometimes they use measures of homesickness that consist of a response to a single test item. Although multiple studies on homesickness have been published, conclusions about the topic remain tentative. The failure to consistently define and measure the construct of homesickness is surely a contributing factor.

Discussion Questions

1. How would you define and measure homesickness? How would you validate a test that measures homesickness?

2. Childhood fears are common, but when they are severe or pervasive they can be very distressing. Use this example, or any other example, of a common problem that, in more extreme forms, is debilitating. Following the example of temper tantrums, how would you study this problem? What kinds of psychological tests would you use to conduct your research?

3. Diener et al. (1985) found a way to measure satisfaction with life using only five questions. How would you go about measuring gratitude, another aspect of positive psychology? How could you measure changes in gratitude after an intervention intended to increase the frequency of feelings of gratitude in daily life? How would you validate your measure of gratitude?

Research Ideas

1. Choose a widely used psychological test such as the MMPI-2, the Wechsler Adult Intelligence Scale-IV, or the Beck Depression Inventory. Consider how the test has been used to advance one or more areas of study in psychology. In addition, discuss how researchers addressed issues of reliability and validity in their research and research reports.

2. Imagine this line of research: Alcohol consumption in college students following an intervention targeting problem drinking in underage students. How would you determine if a psychological test suggested for this study is a good method of obtaining data? As part of the discussion, review and critique psychological tests that measure substance use.

3. Review research on procrastination. What measures have been used in this line of research? How would you measure procrastination in college students? How would you validate the tests you plan to use in your study?

References

Burtt, H. E., & Arps, G. F. (1920, December). Correlation of Army intelligence test with academic grades in high schools and military academies. *Journal of Applied Psychology, 4*(4), 289–293.

Diener, E., Emmons, R. A., Larsen, R. J., & Griffin, S. (1985, February). The satisfaction with life scale. *Journal of Personality Assessment, 49*(1), 71–75.

Irons, J. G., Bassett, D. T., Prendergast, C. O., Landrum, R. E., & Heinz, A. J. (2016). Development and initial validation of the caffeine consumption questionnaire–revised. *Journal of Caffeine Research, 6*(1), 20–25.

Larsen, J. T., & McKibban, A. R. (2008). Is happiness having what you want or wanting what you have, or both? *Psychological Science, 19*(4), 371–377.

Open Science Collaboration. (2015, August 28). Estimating the reproducibility of psychological science. *Science, 349*(6251), aac4716. doi:10.1126/science.aac4716

Rozental, A., Forsell, E., Svensson, A., Andersson, G., & Carlbring, P. (2015). Internet-based cognitive—behavior therapy for procrastination: A randomized controlled trial. *Journal of Consulting and Clinical Psychology, 83*(4), 808–824. Retrieved from http://dx.doi.org/10.1037/ccp0000023

Seibel, L., Vermue, M., van Dooren, R., Kolorz, F. M., Cillessen, L., & Krause, R. W. (2015, August 19). Replication of Larsen & McKibban (Psych Science, 2008, Exp. 2). Retrieved from osf.io/5dx4v

Stroebe, M., Schut, H., & Nauta, M. (2015). Homesickness: A systematic review of the scientific literature. *Review of General Psychology, 19*(2), 157–171. Retrieved from http://dx.doi.org/10.1037/gpr0000037

Thurber, C. A. (1995). The experience and expression of homesickness in preadolescent and adolescent boys. *Child Development, 66*(4), 1162–1178.

Thurber, C. A. (2005). Multimodal homesickness prevention in boys spending 2 weeks at a residential summer camp. *Journal of Consulting and Clinical Psychology, 73*(3), 555–560. doi:10.1037/0022-006X.73.3.555

Thurber, C. A., & Sigman, M. D. (1998). Preliminary models of risk and protective factors for childhood homesickness: Review and empirical synthesis. *Child Development, 69*(4), 903–934.

Vanhalst, J., Soenens, B., Luyckx, K., Van Petegem, S., Weeks, M. S., & Asher, S. R. (2015). Why do the lonely stay lonely? Chronically lonely adolescents' attributions and emotions in situations of social inclusion and exclusion. *Journal of Personality and Social Psychology, 109*(5), 932–948. Retrieved from http://dx.doi.org/10.1037/pspp0000051

Wakschlag, L. S., Briggs-Gowan, M. J., Choi, S. W., Nichols, S. R., Kestler, J., Burns, J. L., Carter, A. S., & Henry, D. (2014, January). Advancing a multidimensional, developmental spectrum approach to preschool disruptive behavior. *Journal of the American Academy of Child & Adolescent Psychiatry, 53*(1), 82–96.

Wakschlag, L. S., Briggs-Gowan, M. J., Tolan, P., Hill, C., Danis, B., & Carter, A. (2010). *The multidimensional assessment of preschool disruptive behavior (MAP-DB) questionnaire.* Unpublished measure.

Wakschlag, L. S., Choi, S. W., Carter, A. S., Hullsiek, H., Burns, J., McCarthy, K., Leibenluft, E., & Briggs-Gowan, M. J. (2012, November). Defining the developmental parameters of temper loss in early childhood: Implications for developmental psychopathology. *Journal of Child Psychology and Psychiatry, 53*(11), 1099–1108.

5

PSYCHOLOGICAL TESTING IN MENTAL HEALTH DIAGNOSIS AND TREATMENT

LEARNING OBJECTIVES

- Describe two approaches to using psychological tests in the treatment of mental health problems

- Identify three controversies related to using psychological tests in mental health settings

- Discuss the relationship between psychological test results and mental health diagnoses

- Compare the goals of therapeutic assessment and outcomes assessment

Derrick is 6 years old. He has been acting up in school, he is difficult to manage at home, and he is much more active than his older sisters were at his age. His parents weren't too concerned about his behavior until they got another call from his school, this time from the principal. They decided to talk with his pediatrician. She told them that Derrick might have ADHD, and she asked both parents to fill out a questionnaire about Derrick's behavior and to bring a questionnaire to school for Derrick's teacher to complete.

This scenario takes place every day in pediatricians' offices, child therapists' offices, and in child and family clinics and agencies. Derrick's parents would probably be asked to complete a behavior rating scale, such as the Conners-3 Parent Report (Conners, 2009). The Conners-3 is a norm-referenced behavior rating scale in which someone who knows a child well responds to a lot of very specific questions about the child's behavior. Results are tabulated and compared to normative data, which are the results for other children of the same age. Scores that are higher than average, to a statistically significant degree, suggest the child has certain kinds of behaviors or other problems that are atypical. The clinician uses the test data as part of an assessment that usually includes gathering background information as well as a review of symptoms.

Many different kinds of psychological tests are used in mental health settings to diagnose mental health conditions, to plan treatment, and to evaluate treatment outcomes. However, psychological tests are not used for every client or by every clinician, and the use of psychological tests in clinical settings is not an area of settled practice. Some clinicians believe tests should not be used at all in clinical settings, that they add no value and could misinform treatment efforts, while others believe that more clients would benefit from testing than currently receive it.

Behavior rating scales, such as the Conners-3, make it easier to determine whether behavior is developmentally typical, an important issue in child assessment. Cognitive ability tests, such as the Wechsler Intelligence Scale for Children-V (WISC-V) and the Wechsler Adult Intelligence Scale-IV (WAIS-IV), are often necessary when determining if an individual has an intellectual disability but are also used in the assessment of learning disabilities and in treatment planning. Broad self-report tests of personality and emotional functioning, such as the MMPI-2 and Personality Assessment Inventory (PAI), are used by some clinicians to assess clients before deciding on a diagnosis and treatment plan. Narrow self-report tests that assess specific problem areas, such as the Beck Depression Inventory-II (BDI-II), are more commonly used by clinicians. They can be used to determine the presence of a specific mental health condition and its severity and to track the severity of the condition over treatment. Performance based, or projective, tests are those that require the test taker to engage in an activity, such as the Rorschach Inkblot Method (Rorschach), during which test takers describe what an inkblot might be. These kinds of tests are much more controversial. There are serious disagreements between psychologists about whether projective tests provide useful information about personality, emotional functioning, mental health diagnosis, or anything else. However, regarding the Rorschach specifically, psychologists have come to agree, based on research findings, that at minimum, test results are valid for determining the presence of thought disorder, a symptom of Schizophrenia and some other types of serious mental illness (Wood, Garb, Nezworski, Lilienfeld, & Duke, 2015).

In a recent survey, it was found that "a large majority of psychologists believe psychological assessment is a valuable aid in making diagnostic decisions and treatment recommendations" (Wright et al., 2016, p. 5). However, 20% of practicing psychologists who responded to the survey don't conduct any testing at all in their practices.

This chapter describes the uses of psychological testing in treating mental health conditions. It also describes controversies that have consumed the field for many years. Some of the controversies have to do with the psychometric properties of tests, while others are concerned with the nature of clinical practice and the relevance of testing to the clinical setting.

ASSESSMENT AND TREATMENT OF MENTAL HEALTH PROBLEMS

Mental health settings address the needs of people who have behavioral, emotional, or thinking problems that result in personal distress or impaired functioning. These are considered mental health problems and include an extraordinarily broad group of challenges, from very narrow behavior problems such as Trichitillomania (pulling out one's hair) to mood disorders such as depression, and problems in thinking that characterize psychotic disorders such as Schizophrenia. Bipolar Disorder, Obsessive-Compulsive Disorder (OCD), Attention Deficit Hyperactivity Disorder (ADHD), and Schizophrenia are mental disorders that most people have heard of.

The *Diagnostic and Statistical Manual* (DSM), a publication of the American Psychiatric Association (2013) identifies, describes, and classifies mental health problems or mental disorders. The DSM is currently in its 5th edition and is known as DSM-5. The World Health Organization (WHO) (1993) also classifies mental disorders. Both classification systems describe specific mental disorders and the symptoms that characterize them so that, to the extent possible given available data, clinicians can provide accurate and consistent diagnoses based on scientific evidence.

Not everyone who has a mental disorder receives treatment and even fewer people receive treatment in a mental health setting, such as a psychiatric clinic, hospital, or private practice. Many people are diagnosed with and treated for mental disorders by primary care physicians. The reverse is also true; some people who seek help in a mental health setting have family, relationship, or work problems and don't have any diagnosable mental disorders.

With few exceptions, mental disorders cannot be diagnosed by blood tests, brain scans, or other techniques used in physical medicine. Instead, they are diagnosed by observation and the patient's report of signs and symptoms, sometimes with the help of information provided by family members, or through school, legal, or medical records. For example, Major Depressive Disorder, the most common mental disorder according to the Centers for Disease Control (CDC), is diagnosed based on the presence of disturbances in mood, sleep, appetite, interest and pleasure in activities, ability to concentrate, energy level, view of the self, and thoughts of death or suicidal ideation. Not all of the symptoms have to be present to warrant a diagnosis of depression, but a number of them must be present for at least a two-week period, and during that period the individual must have a low mood or a loss of interest or pleasure in activities for most of the two-week period. Every disorder in the DSM-5 has a list of signs and symptoms, or diagnostic criteria, that are the hallmarks of the disorder and that mental health clinicians rely on to make psychiatric diagnoses. Individuals often have signs and symptoms of more than one mental disorder.

Mental health diagnoses are made by physicians and similar health care professionals, and they are also made by specialists in mental health, such as psychologists, social workers, and counselors. Although some mental health professionals use rating scales or simple questionnaires when making a diagnosis, this is far from standard practice, and psychological testing is often not part of the diagnostic or treatment process at all.

THE ROLE OF PSYCHOLOGICAL TESTING IN THE MENTAL HEALTH SETTING

Although they are not routinely used in mental health treatment, psychological tests can serve a number of important functions in addressing mental health related problems. They can

- provide a format for reporting symptoms of mental disorders and their severity;
- provide score profiles of individuals known to have a disorder to compare with score profiles of the patient;
- provide a context for the interpretation of signs and symptoms;
- provide an understanding of personality factors that affect how a patient exhibits signs and symptoms;
- contribute to an evaluation of risk of violence or suicide;
- contribute to treatment and to treatment planning; and
- measure treatment progress and outcome.

In mental health settings, psychological tests might be a simple addition to an initial evaluation, a quick way to assess the severity of a client's depression. In other circumstances, a client who has complex challenges might be referred to an assessment psychologist for a formal, comprehensive psychological assessment, a practice that involves interviewing the client, administering tests, and integrating test data with data gathered in other ways.

PSYCHOLOGICAL TESTS USED IN MENTAL HEALTH SETTINGS: A HISTORY

Although it seems unlikely, many of the tests that are commonly used in mental health settings today were initially conceived many years ago. For example, in 1905, with a colleague, Alfred Binet developed a scale to measure intelligence, the Binet-Simon Scale. The scale included multiple tasks, each including items of increasing difficulty. Intelligence tests in use today are similarly constructed. In 1921, Hermann Rorschach developed the inkblot test that is still used by psychologists around the world, known as the Rorschach Psychodiagnostic Technique. The test is administered and scored differently than it once was, but the inkblots themselves haven't changed. Work on the MMPI, mentioned previously, was started in 1939 at the University of Minnesota. The purpose of the MMPI when it was first developed was to evaluate patients in psychiatric care and determine the severity of their problems. The MMPI in its latest versions, the MMPI-2 and a shorter form, the MMPI-2 RF, are still used to assist in diagnosing mental health problems, but its use has expanded to include examining personality characteristics and other aspects of individual functioning. Many new tests have been developed as well, including symptom based self-report tests, structured and semistructured interviews to diagnose specific disorders, behavior rating scales, and computer administered tests of attention.

Administering a group, or battery, of tests that includes global measures of intellectual functioning and personality continues to be important in some settings (see Bram & Peebles, 2014). Other situations call for the use of a single test or a small group of tests to assess the presence and severity of specific problems or to measure global outcomes. Regardless of the setting, in order to provide effective services psychologists who conduct assessments must choose tests wisely, use tests that are well supported by research, interpret test results accurately, and thoughtfully integrate test data with other clinical information.

ISSUES AND CONTROVERSIES

Although psychological tests contribute to the diagnosis and treatment of mental disorders, their use is controversial. For example, psychologists have been relying on test batteries, groups of tests used together, to conduct psychological assessments of psychiatric patients since at least the 1940s, when David Rapaport and his colleagues published a manual supporting the use of a test battery in evaluating patients with mental health conditions (Rapaport, Gill, & Schafer, 1946; Rapaport, Gill, and Schafer, 1968). Although academic psychologists were not supportive of the method, as was evident in multiple reviews in academic journals at the time (e.g., Lindner, 1946), clinical psychologists who worked with patients in treatment settings found Rapaport's approach invaluable. Many still do (Bram & Peebles, 2014; Carlson, 2013).

Academic psychologists were concerned about the quality of the data presented by Rapaport and colleagues in support of their efforts, an ongoing issue. Some psychologists continue to try to demonstrate the value of psychological assessment by collecting and presenting data (Meyer et al., 2001), while others are highly critical of their efforts (Lilienfeld, Garb, & Wood, 2011). The criticism is based in part on questioning the validity of the tests themselves, particularly the Rorschach and other projective tests, and in part on questioning whether additional tests, or in some cases, any tests, add anything of value to the assessment and treatment process. A focus on evidence-based assessment and treatment and all of the controversies over the validity of the Rorschach have made for tests that are psychometrically stronger and a push to use these tests over others that are not as well supported by research. Even the Rorschach has been made more psychometrically sound through a review of validity studies (Mihura, Meyer, Dumitrascu, & Bombel, 2013) and through the development of a new approach to administering, scoring, and interpreting test results, the Rorschach Performance Assessment System or R-PAS (Meyer, Viglione, Mihura, Erard, & Erdberg, 2011).

Another criticism of psychological assessment, which typically relies on a psychologist to exercise judgment and pull together different sources of information, is related to a famous dispute about the merits of statistical versus clinical prediction of future behavior. In 1954, Paul Meehl published an influential monograph, or brief book, focused on the advantages of statistical prediction through use of an algorithm over clinical prediction based on clinical judgment. In reviewing numerous studies, he determined that statistical prediction was always as good as, if not better than, clinical judgment in predicting future behavior, a key goal of mental health assessment. However, psychologists working with patients didn't change their practices in line with Meehl's results. The issues continue to be debated (Grove & Vrieze, 2009). As Horn, Mihura, and Meyer (2013) point out, the goal of assessment in a clinical context is not to predict behavior but to describe an individual. They also note that algorithms do not exist for most of the circumstances requiring clinical judgment in assessment situations.

A third controversy stems from the debate over the role of situational factors versus personality traits in determining behavior. In 1968, Walter Mischel published *Personality and Assessment*, an examination of the role of situational factors versus enduring personality traits. If behavior is situation specific, then why assess personality at all? Along the same lines, behaviorally oriented psychologists plan treatment to help their clients change behavior, focusing on observable behaviors, and they view psychological testing as irrelevant to their efforts.

BEST PRACTICES IN PSYCHOLOGICAL ASSESSMENT IN MENTAL HEALTH SETTINGS

Current best practice is to use psychological assessment to answer specific referral questions (Horn et al., 2013), rather than to routinely use the same battery of psychological tests to inform the treatment of all patients. An assessment psychologist might evaluate a client referred by her therapist to rule out an underlying thought disorder, a problem related to serious mental illness, because the client has unusual thought patterns and the therapist is uncertain about their origins. A client who is underachieving in school might be referred for evaluation to find out why she is having so much academic trouble. Does she have a learning disability, or is her depression causing the problem?

For example, Ariana is a (fictitious) 21-year-old who was placed on academic probation at her university due to poor grades. She had been working with a therapist for about six months to address her low mood, but it didn't seem to make a difference in her academic progress. Her therapist referred her to a colleague to evaluate her for ADHD and other learning problems. The psychologist conducting the assessment interviewed Ariana, her mother, and the therapist. She administered cognitive ability and academic achievement tests; a personality test with scales measuring ADHD, depression, and anxiety; and two projective tests. She chose these tests because there were multiple competing explanations for Ariana's academic problems. The psychologist scored and interpreted all of the tests and wrote a report with the findings and recommendations to share with Ariana, her parents, and her therapist.

In the report, the psychologist concluded that Ariana was struggling with depression, a reading disorder, and some family problems, all of which needed to be addressed for Ariana to succeed in school. She made detailed treatment recommendations and also recommended, in a separate report to be shared with Ariana's college, academic accommodations and specific types of academic support. She was able to document the need for accommodations through Ariana's test scores and history.

OUTCOMES ASSESSMENT

One special role psychological testing serves in mental health settings is outcomes assessment, the assessment of treatment results for individuals or groups. Outcomes assessment can focus on a patient's symptoms, capacity to function, subjective sense of well-being, or on all of these outcomes. It can help individual clinicians, as well as organizations, improve the quality of care they provide to patients. Although there is an increasing demand for outcomes assessment as well as recognition of its value (Maruish, 2013), outcomes assessment is used by less than half of practicing psychologists (Hatfield & Ogles, 2004). A recent survey of Canadian psychologists indicates that very few use psychological tests to monitor treatment progress, 12%. Instead, most practitioners rely on clinical judgment to determine patient progress (Ionita & Fitzpatrick, 2014).

Those clinicians who do outcomes assessment use both patient and clinician report measures, with patient self-report measures most common (Farnsworth, Hess, & Lambert, 2001). The basic method of outcomes assessment is to engage in repeated measurement of symptoms, general distress, quality of life, capacity to function, or any other target of treatment. The measurements can be taken at various times, including prior to initiating treatment, at the end of treatment, and months after treatment is over. Outcomes assessment can answer several questions including how much change occurred in treatment, which aspect of treatment contributed to change, and how to improve the treatment services delivered by individual providers or an organization.

The choice of measures for outcomes assessment depends on its goals. Self-report measures focused on symptoms of specific disorders, such as the Beck Depression Inventory–II (BDI), tend to be brief and easy for patients to complete, but they may not be as reliable as more general measures of symptoms and distress, and they can miss important changes. Broad measures, such as the MMPI-2, are burdensome for clients to complete. Other measures used in outcomes assessment include measures of quality of life, such as the Quality of Life Inventory, or measures of functioning, such as the Katz Adjustment Scales. Still other outcome measures include clinician ratings or ratings by significant others in the patient's life, such as parents or a spouse.

Several measures, and measurement systems, have been specifically developed to monitor treatment progress and outcomes. The Outcomes Questionnaire-45 (OQ-45) is one example. Developed by Dr. Michael Lambert, the OQ-45 is a self-report measure of symptom distress, relationship problems, and social roles. It takes only a few minutes to complete and can be administered repeatedly, with the initial administration intended to be prior to the initial session.

The data obtained in outcomes assessment is interpreted through statistical techniques that focus on clinically significant changes in scores for individuals or statistically significant differences between the mean scores of groups of individuals. Then the findings are communicated to stakeholders.

Outcomes assessment has a lot of potential for improving treatment, but McAleavey and colleagues (McAleavey, Nordberg, Kraus, & Castonguay, 2012) note that, similar to other psychological test uses, measurement for the purpose of outcomes assessment is vulnerable to error. Change can be detected falsely. For example, change can be attributed to treatment effectiveness when it is temporary and circumstantial, or beneficial changes might not be detected when they have occurred. Also, patients may interpret individual test items idiosyncratically, distorting the interpretation of test results.

THERAPEUTIC ASSESSMENT

Finally, therapeutic assessment (TA) is one of the newest and most promising approaches to using psychological tests in mental health settings. It is different than other uses of psychological tests because TA is a form of treatment, not assessment. It is used on its own as an intervention or as a supplement to other treatment. TA uses a wide variety of tests depending on the circumstances and often employs a group of tests similar to those used by Rapaport and colleagues (1968), perhaps with some additions. The goal of TA is to help clients solve problems by making use of insights provided through interpretation of psychological tests. TA has been shown to be effective relative to other treatment approaches for college students, inpatients, families, and children with oppositional defiant disorder (see Finn & Martin, 2013). However, much work remains to be done to firmly establish TA as an evidence-based practice.

EVALUATING DERRICK FOR ADHD: A BRIEF CASE EXAMPLE

Derrick's parents completed the Connors-3 parent rating forms, and they asked Derrick's teacher to complete a teacher's version of the form as well. All three produced valid profiles, and all three profiles included elevations in the Mildly Atypical range for Inattention and in the Moderately Atypical range for Hyperactivity. The pediatrician also asked Derrick's parents a lot of questions about his behavior at home and how things were going for the family, and she asked if anyone in the family was treated for ADHD or had similar problems. She found out that Derrick's father had similar behavior problems in school when he was growing up, as did Derrick's uncle. She already knew Derrick's early developmental history from his medical records. She also observed him in the office, and she asked him some questions too. She also asked his parents to bring in his progress reports from school and any other school records. The pediatrician was trying to learn more about Derrick's attention and hyperactivity issues, and she wanted to make sure there were no other problems that would account for them.

She concluded that Derrick had ADHD with both inattention and hyperactivity. He was young to make the diagnosis, but all of the information she had was consistent, and he was having a lot of problems with self-control in school. She knew it was important to address them. She talked with his parents about the diagnosis and treatment options. They decided to see a child psychologist who specialized in ADHD in young children and not to start Derrick on medication just yet, although they planned to keep that option open.

CONCLUSION

Psychological tests are used for all clients, for some clients, or not at all in mental health settings, depending on the setting and the clinician. Their use can be controversial. Even the use of rating scales in child assessment, such as the rating scale used by Derrick's pediatrician in the example above, although quite common, is not consistent across mental health providers.

When they are used in mental health treatment, psychological tests serve a number of different functions. In TA, insights gained from psychological testing are used collaboratively with a client as a form of treatment, and in outcomes assessment psychological tests are used to determine progress in treatment.

Individual psychological tests are also used in a battery of tests to understand patients, make diagnoses, and plan treatment. This approach was developed in the 1940s and it continues to be employed today, for all clients in some settings and for some clients in other settings. Perhaps more frequently, psychological tests are used to measure symptoms and symptom severity for purposes of diagnosis and treatment planning, often relying on one or a small group of measures focused on measuring specific kinds of problems, such as depression, OCD, or ADHD.

Discussion Questions

1. Should therapists use outcome measures in their practices? Why or why not?

2. How should controversies among clinical psychologists be resolved?

3. In what circumstances would psychological testing for clients with mental health disorders be considered evidence-based assessment?

4. What guidelines should be followed in deciding whether or not to refer a client for psychological testing?

Research Ideas

1. Review the history of the MMPI, the MMPI-2, and the MMPI-2 RF, and discuss changes in how they have been used in mental health treatment through the years. Discuss the future of the MMPI in mental health care.

2. Review the literature on therapeutic assessment for adults and discuss the circumstances in which therapeutic assessment qualifies as evidence-based treatment.

3. What psychological tests are used in the assessment of ADHD and for what purpose?

References

American Psychiatric Association. (2013). *Diagnostic and Statistical Manual for Mental Disorders* (5th edition). Washington, DC: Author.

Bram, A. D., & Peebles, M. J. (2014). *Psychological testing that matters: Creating a road map for effective treatment*. Washington, DC: American Psychological Association.

Carlson, J. F. (2013). Clinical and counseling testing. In K. F. Geisinger, B. A. Bracken, J. F. Carlson, J-I. C. Hansen, N. R. Kuncel, S. P. Reise, & M. C. Rodriguez (Eds.), *APA handbook of testing and assessment in psychology, Vol. 2: Testing and assessment in clinical and counseling psychology* (pp. 3–17). Washington, DC: American

Psychological Association. Retrieved from http://dx.doi.org/10.1037/14048-001

Conners, C. K. (2009). *Conners 3rd edition manual*. North Tonawanda, NY: Multihealth Systems.

Farnsworth, J. R., Hess, J. Z., & Lambert, M. J. (2001, August). *Frequency of outcome measures used in psychotherapy*. Poster presented at the 109th Annual Convention of the American Psychological Association, San Francisco, CA.

Finn, S. E., & Martin, H. (2013). Therapeutic assessment: Using psychological testing as brief therapy. In K. F. Geisinger, B. A. Bracken, J. F. Carlson, J-I. C. Hansen, N. R. Kuncel, S. P. Reise, & M. C. Rodriguez (Eds.), *APA handbook of testing and assessment in psychology, Vol. 2: Testing and assessment in clinical and counseling psychology* (pp. 453–465). Washington, DC: American Psychological Association. Retrieved from http://dx.doi.org/10.1037/14048-026

Grove, W. M., & Vrieze, S. I. (2013). The clinical versus mechanical prediction controversy. In K. F. Geisinger, B. A. Bracken, J. F. Carlson, J-I. C. Hansen, N. R. Kuncel, S. P. Reise, & M. C. Rodriguez (Eds.), *APA handbook of testing and assessment in psychology, Vol. 2: Testing and assessment in clinical and counseling psychology* (pp. 51–62). Washington, DC: American Psychological Association. Retrieved from http://psycnet.apa.org/record/2012-22486-004

Hatfield, D. R., & Ogles, B. M. (2004). The use of outcome measures by psychologists in clinical practice. *Professional Psychology: Research and Practice, 35*(5), 485–491. doi:10.1037/0735-7028.35.5.485

Horn, S. L., Mihura, J. L., & Meyer, G. J. (2013). Psychological assessment in adult mental health settings. In K. F. Geisinger, B. A. Bracken, J. F. Carlson, J-I. C. Hansen, N. R. Kuncel, S. P. Reise, & M. C. Rodriguez (Eds.), *APA handbook of testing and assessment in psychology, Vol. 2: Testing and assessment in clinical and counseling psychology* (pp. 231–252). Washington, DC: American Psychological Association. Retrieved from http://dx.doi.org/10.1037/14048-014

Ionita, G., & Fitzpatrick, M. (2014). Bringing science to clinical practice: A Canadian survey of psychological practice and usage of progress monitoring measures. *Canadian Psychology/Psychologie Canadienne, 55*(3), 187–196. doi:10.1037/a0037355

Lilienfeld, S. O., Garb, H. N., & Wood, J. M. (2011). Unresolved questions concerning the effectiveness of psychological assessment as a therapeutic intervention: Comment on Poston and Hanson (2010). *Psychological Assessment, 23*(4), 1047–1055. doi:10.1037/a0025177

Lindner, R. M. (1946, September). Review of diagnostic psychological testing, vol. II. *Psychological Bulletin, 43*(5), 479–481. Retrieved from http://dx.doi.org/10.1037/h0052598

Maruish, M. E. (2013). Outcome assessment in health settings. In K. F. Geisinger, B. A. Bracken, J. F. Carlson, J-I. C. Hansen, N. R. Kuncel, S. P. Reise, & M. C. Rodriguez (Eds.), *APA handbook of testing and assessment in psychology, Vol. 2: Testing and assessment in clinical and counseling psychology* (pp. 303–321). Washington, DC: American Psychological Association. Retrieved from http://psycnet.apa.org/record/2012-22486-018

McAleavey, A. A., Nordberg, S. S., Kraus, D., & Castonguay, L. G. (2012, May). Errors in treatment outcome monitoring: Implications for real-world psychotherapy. *Canadian Psychology/Psychologie Canadienne, 53*(2), 105–114. doi:10.1037/a0027833

Meehl, P. E. (1954). *Clinical vs statistical prediction: A theoretical analysis and a review of the evidence*. Minneapolis: University of Minnesota Press.

Meyer, G. J., Finn, S. E., Eyde, L. D., Kay, G. G., Moreland, K. L., Dies, R. R., . . . & Reed, G. M. (2001). Psychological testing and psychological assessment: A review of evidence and issues. *American Psychologist, 56*(2), 128–165. Retrieved from http://dx.doi.org/10.1037/0003-066X.56.2.128

Meyer, G. J., Viglione, D. J., Mihura, J. L., Erard, R. E., & Erdberg, P. (2011). *Rorschach performance assessment system: Administration, coding, interpretation, and technical manual*. Toledo, OH: Rorschach Performance Assessment System, LLC.

Mihura, J. L., Meyer, G. J., Dumitrascu, N., & Bombel, G. (2013). The validity of individual Rorschach variables: Systematic reviews and meta-analyses of the comprehensive system. *Psychological Bulletin, 139*(3), 548–605. doi:10.1037/a0029406

Mischel, W. (1968). *Personality and assessment.* Hoboken, NJ: John Wiley.

Rapaport, D., Gill, M., & Schafer, R. (1946). *Diagnostic psychological testing: The theory, statistical evaluation, and diagnostic application of a battery of tests, vol. II.* Chicago, IL: Year Book Publishers.

Rapaport, D., Gill, M., & Schafer, R. (1968). *Diagnostic psychological testing (Rev. ed.),* New York, NY: International Universities Press.

Wood, J. M., Garb, H. N., Nezworski, M. T., Lilienfeld, S. O., & Duke, M. C. (2015). A second look at the validity of widely used Rorschach indices: Comment on Mihura, Meyer, Dumitrascu, and Bombel (2013). *Psychological Bulletin, 141*(1), 236–249.

World Health Organization. (1993). *International classification of diseases, Tenth revision, Clinical modification (ICD-10-CM).* (10th ed.). Retrieved from https://www.cdc.gov/nchs/icd/icd10cm.htm

Wright, C. V., Beattie, S. G., Galpher, D. I., Church, A. S., Bufka, L. F., Brabender, V. M., & Smith, B. L. (2017). Professional psychology. *Research and Practice, 48*(2), 73–78.

6

PSYCHOLOGICAL TESTING IN MEDICINE

Psychological Evaluation Prior to Bariatric Surgery

LEARNING OBJECTIVES

- Explain the importance of using test scores normed on bariatric surgery patients to interpret test results of bariatric surgery clients

- Describe the goals of presurgical evaluation of bariatric surgery patients

- Identify the advantages of including psychological testing in presurgical evaluation of bariatric surgery patients

- Describe factors that should be considered in choosing psychological tests to use in the presurgical evaluation of bariatric surgery patients

Joanne is a married mother of two young adults who live on their own. She works as a school secretary. She has been gradually putting on weight since she became pregnant with her first child more than 26 years ago. She has Type 2 diabetes and high blood pressure, and at her last physical, she weighed more than she ever did before at 200 lbs. Her doctor told her that her Body Mass Index (BMI) was 36, a level categorized as obese. He also told her that with her comorbid medical conditions, diabetes and hypertension, she was a candidate for bariatric surgery, a surgical intervention to help her lose weight.

Like so many of her friends and relatives, Joanne has been dieting on and off for years. She also walks at the high school track a few times a week. She periodically loses weight, but she always gains it back. She researched some new medications that were approved by the Federal Drug Administration for weight loss, but she was leery about the side effects. Worried about her health and unhappy with how she looks and feels, she decides to think seriously about having bariatric surgery if it would help her lose weight and keep it off for good.

PSYCHOLOGICAL TESTING IN MEDICINE

Health care is an enormous field, important in every stage of human life from beginning to end. Considering the scope of the field, psychological testing is infrequently used in the treatment of medical conditions, with the exception of behavioral health. However, there are a few areas of medicine in which psychological tests are commonly employed, although perhaps not in every case. Psychological tests can be helpful in evaluating patients who have problems with chronic pain. They also contribute to medical decision making and planning in select circumstances, such as gender transitioning medical care and in presurgical screening before organ transplants, spine surgery, and bariatric surgery. This chapter examines how and why psychological tests are used prior to bariatric surgery, a common procedure in the treatment of obesity.

THE PROBLEM OF OBESITY

Joanne, the fictitious bariatric surgery candidate described above, is in good company. Obesity is a significant public health problem, not only in the United States but around the world. According to the World Health Organization (WHO), more than 500 million people around the world are obese, 11% of adults. In the United States, more than 36% of adults are obese, based on data from 2011 to 2014 (Ogden, Carroll, Fryar, & Flegal, 2015). Obesity is considered a public health problem because it is a major risk factor for diseases including diabetes, cardiovascular disease, osteoarthritis, and some cancers.

Obesity is a progressive condition that develops over time when individuals take in more calories than they use. Environmental factors such as large portion sizes, high calorie foods, decreases in everyday physical activity, and promotion of less healthy foods through advertising (Centers for Disease Control and Prevention, 2017) contribute to the problem. Personal factors such as genetics, medication side effects, and mental health conditions (for example, depression, impulsivity related to Attention Deficit Hyperactivity Disorder, and binge eating disorder) also contribute to obesity. Making the problem of obesity more challenging, as almost everyone who has tried to lose weight knows, it is hard to lose weight, and it is even harder to maintain weight loss. Weight loss is important from a public health perspective because, even when an individual remains significantly overweight, losing weight reduces risk factors for disease.

The initial treatment of obesity is usually behavioral, making changes in one's diet and activity level. If behavioral approaches aren't effective, medical interventions, including medication and bariatric surgery, are considered. Research has demonstrated that bariatric surgery is both clinically effective and cost effective for the treatment of obesity in moderately to severely obese adults as compared to other interventions (Picot et al., 2009).

BARIATRIC SURGERY: HISTORY AND PURPOSE

Medical interventions for obesity became available early in the 20th century, when doctors began prescribing medication for the condition. Surgery for weight loss was first developed in the 1950's and became increasingly popular in the 1990s. Now, it is a common procedure.

Adults who have a BMI of 30 or more are considered obese, and those adults who have a BMI of 40 or more are considered severely obese. BMI is a calculation of weight divided by height squared. Current treatment guidelines developed by National Institutes of Health (NIH) support bariatric surgery for individuals who have BMIs ≥ 40 or ≥ 35 if they have two or more comorbid health conditions such as diabetes, heart disease, hypertension, or sleep apnea (American Society for Metabolic and Bariatric Surgery, 2017; National Guideline Clearinghouse, 2008).

Bariatric surgery is a general term that refers to surgery for the purpose of weight loss. Gastric bypass surgery is one type of bariatric surgery procedure. It restricts the amount of food the stomach can hold. Other types of bariatric surgery work by lowering the absorption rate of calories and nutrients. Still others combine techniques to both restrict the amount of food the stomach can hold and lower the absorption rate of calories and nutrients. All require significant preparation and lifestyle changes during and after the recovery period.

THE GOALS OF PRESURGICAL PSYCHOLOGICAL EVALUATION

Presurgical psychological evaluation of bariatric surgery candidates has been recommended by the NIH and other organizations since at least the early 1990s (see Marek et al., 2016). Formal clinical practice guidelines specifically call for presurgical psychosocial evaluation, among other screening procedures, as described below:

> A psychosocial-behavioral evaluation, which assesses environmental, familial, and behavioral factors, should be required for all patients before bariatric surgery. . . . Any patient considered for bariatric surgery with a known or suspected psychiatric illness, or substance abuse, or dependence, should undergo a formal mental health evaluation before performance of the surgical procedure. (Mechanick et al., 2013)

Presurgical psychological evaluation covers all of these concerns.

Bariatric surgery patients face significant dietary restrictions, pre- and post-operatively. They also face emotional challenges and relationship issues post-operatively, given the expectations for change following surgery and the realistic challenges of living with change (Meana & Ricciardi, 2008). Psychological evaluation can identify eating disorders, emotional problems, and relationship issues that could put weight loss and maintenance of weight loss after surgery at risk. It also provides an opportunity for educating patients about bariatric surgery and helps ensure that patients make well-informed decisions about undertaking the surgery, are prepared for it, and have realistic expectations.

Another purpose of presurgical psychological evaluation is to identify patients who are poor candidates for surgery due to psychiatric problems, substance abuse, or cognitive dysfunction and to assist with educating and planning for this group of patients. Patients who are not considered good candidates for surgery following evaluation often benefit from undergoing mental health treatment and good planning for post-operative care, and thus, they become good candidates for surgery. The option of surgery is not closed permanently in most cases (Marcus et al., 2009).

Psychological evaluation prior to surgery can promote positive outcomes from surgery in addition to reducing risk. Bariatric surgery patients need to continue with dietary restrictions and increased activity for the remainder of their lives to have the best outcomes from surgery: significant weight loss, maintenance of weight loss, and improved quality of life. Depression, poor impulse control, interpersonal problems including low levels of social support, untreated eating disorders, and stress can interfere with having the best outcomes from surgery, and patients benefit if plans are put in place to manage these kinds of problems post-operatively.

SELECTING AND ADMINISTERING PSYCHOLOGICAL TESTS TO PROSPECTIVE BARIATRIC SURGERY PATIENTS

Presurgical psychological evaluations with the dual goals of preventing negative outcomes and promoting positive outcomes after bariatric surgery include an interview with a mental health provider, and in most instances, the administration of one or more psychological tests (Fabricatore et al., 2013). According to Sarwer, Allison, Bailer, Faulconbridge, and Wadden (2013), objective measurement, or psychological tests, are used in two thirds of presurgical psychological evaluations of bariatric surgery patients. However, there is no specific, evidence-based protocol for presurgical psychological evaluation, nor are there consensus guidelines for how to conduct the interview or for which tests to include (see Bauchowitz et al., 2005; Heinberg, 2013).

Evaluators typically assess family support; the patient's motivation for surgery; expectations for outcome; psychiatric history (to determine the patient's current psychiatric status and to anticipate psychiatric vulnerabilities in the future); substance abuse history and current use or abuse of drugs and alcohol; whether the patient has an eating disorder, particularly, binge eating disorder or night eating syndrome; and the use of antidepressants (Sarwer et al., 2013). Active substance abuse, untreated psychiatric problems, and eating disorders seriously complicate recovery, and the use of antidepressants can be problematic due to changes in how antidepressants are metabolized after surgery. Patients with these kinds of problems may be able to benefit from surgery, but problems patients exhibit in these areas need to be addressed before surgery and plans need to be made for effective management/intervention post-surgery as well. In addition, the evaluator typically assesses the patient's weight loss and dieting history.

Although there are no consensus guidelines or evidence-based protocols dictating the use of specific, or any, psychological tests in psychological evaluation for prospective bariatric surgery patients, some authors have argued that there are distinct advantages to supplementing an interview with formalized testing. Heinberg (2013) notes, for example, that tests add information to data collected in an interview and allow for individualized recommendations. Tests also can reduce liability as compared to mental health evaluations that involve clinicians making judgments based on interview data alone.

Heinberg (2013) also notes that any psychological test used in mental health evaluation for prospective bariatric surgery patients must have good psychometrics; that is, it must be supported by data indicating its reliability and validity for use in prescreening bariatric surgery patients. It should also have normative data for bariatric patients, and it should incorporate measures of social desirability and other types of distorted responding.

Tests that have been used in the psychological evaluation of bariatric surgery patients include symptom measures, personality measures, measures of eating habits and eating disorders, other measures of specific psychiatric or substance abuse problems, such as screening tests for alcohol problems, and quality of life measures. Marek et al. (2016) recommend that the evaluation include a broad-based instrument that measures personality and emotional functioning as well as narrower measures of mood problems, eating habits, and substance use.

Sogg, Lauretti, and West-Smith (2016), in a report prepared for the American Society for Bariatric Surgery, offer the following considerations in choosing psychological tests to use in the evaluation of prospective bariatric surgery patients:

- The reliability and validity of the measure

- The availability of empirically established, bariatric-specific norms

- The availability of research that shows a relationship between the instrument and the outcome of bariatric surgery

- The importance of the domains measured by the test

- The availability of validity scales and the extent to which test results are affected by self-report bias

- The burden of time, personal intrusiveness, and/or cost that the measure imposes on the patient, program, and/or clinician

- The amount and incremental value of additional information that the measure will provide beyond what can readily and reliably obtained during a clinical interview

Wise and Streiner (2010) note that the most frequently used broadband personality tests for presurgical evaluation are the MMPI-2, PAI, MCMI III, Millon Behavioral Medicine Diagnostic (MBMD), and the Millon Behavioral Health Inventory (MBHI). A broadband personality test refers to a general measure of personality characteristics and/or mental health problems and strengths. They point to the importance of using relevant norms for interpreting test results. The MMPI-2 and the MMPI-2-RF, the PAI, and the MBMD have been normed on bariatric patients, the relevant population for the assessment.

Why is it necessary to use relevant norms? Interpretation of test results may not be accurate if broader norms are used, that is, if test results of the prebariatric surgery patient are compared to test results of other populations or the general population. For example, a patient who is experiencing pain may endorse items that make her look depressed (for example, problems with sleep or keeping one's mind on tasks) when the problem is not depression but pain related to a medical condition. If there aren't norms specific to bariatric surgery patients available for a test, it must be assumed that norms for the general population are appropriate. This is problematic because in at least one study medical outpatients responded differently to the MMPI-2 than people who weren't medical outpatients, the community sample (Colligan et al., 2008).

PSYCHOMETRIC ISSUES

Even when a test has appropriate norms, it may have other psychometric problems. Wise and Streiner (2010) look closely at the MBMD, a test intended to replace the MBHI and by the same authors. They indicate that items on the MBMD scales overlap too much, producing more than one psychometric challenge that the test authors attempt to manage, unsuccessfully, by weighting each item. The test authors also rely on base-rate transformation scores to adjust the scales for the prevalence of problems, but they didn't publicize the base rates they used, in conflict with the Standards of Psychological and Educational Testing (APA, 2014). Wise and Streiner conclude that it is essential to use caution when adopting new instruments, especially if test construction methods are problematic as they are, in Wise and Streiner's opinion, for the MBMD.

Tarescavage, Wygant, Boutacoff, and Ben-Porath (2013, August) support the use of the MMPI-2-RF for presurgical psychological evaluation of bariatric patients and note that the MMPI-2-RF has improved psychometric properties for this population relative to the MMPI-2. The MMPI-2-RF has nine validity scales and 42 substantive scales, and it has comparison groups for male and female bariatric surgery candidates.

Tarescavage et al. (2013, August) examined the convergent and discriminant validity of MMPI-2-RF scale scores for bariatric surgery candidates by calculating correlations with external criteria, such as scores on relevant scales of other instruments. Convergent validity is concerned with whether a measure is related to something it should be related to, while discriminant validity is concerned with whether a measure differs from those it shouldn't be related to. They also calculated relative risk ratios (RRRs) by dividing the risk of a negative outcome for individuals who score at or above a cutoff on a specific MMPI-2-RF scale by the risk of a negative outcome for those who score below the cutoff. They based their results on the scores of 759 protocols of bariatric surgery candidates.

Notable findings of their study include:

- Bariatric patients produce elevated scores on the MLS scale, which measures an overall sense of poor health.

- Mean inter-item correlations and internal consistency estimates indicate generally adequate reliability for the Higher Order, RC, and Personality-Psychopathology-5 Scales of the MMPI-2 RF. In contrast, scales measuring thought dysfunction had lower internal consistency estimates, probably due to range restrictions (thought dysfunction is not a common problem in bariatric surgery patients).

- Some specific problem scales had very low internal consistency estimates but adequate inter-item correlations. This is probably due to the low number of items on the scales.

- Emotional dysfunction domain scales showed good convergent validity with quality of life and health survey measures.

- Scales in the interpersonal functioning domain did not correlate as predicted with external criteria. Also, the somatic/cognitive scales did not correlate as predicted with the health survey results.

- Specific Externalizing scales were correlated with impulsivity leading to overeating. Results support the use of these scales (BXD, RC4, JCP) to identify patients at risk of poor compliance after surgery.

RRR results suggested that lower cutoff scores improved RRRs for some scales. The cutoff for the general population is 65 T. Using cutoff scores that are lower than 65 T may have better clinical utility for bariatric surgery candidates because prospective bariatric surgery patients tend to underreport problems. However, they conclude that more research is needed to support the use of lower cutoff scores.

In another study of the MMPI-2-RF with 1,000 bariatric surgery patients, Tarescavage et al. (2013, December) examined using alternative cutoff scores to maximize the accuracy of scales measuring suicidal/death ideation (SUI) and substance abuse problems (SUB). For the SUI scale, the authors hypothesized that taking out one particular item would lower the false positive rate. This item is concerned with death preoccupation, and obese individuals often experience life-threatening comorbidities that can lead to death preoccupation without suicide risk. For the SUB scale, they hypothesized that lowering the cutoff score would improve the sensitivity of the scale, due to underreporting of symptoms by patients because of their desire to be approved for surgery. They found that removing the one item on the SUI scale led to an improvement in classification, so that 90% of patients were correctly classified. With the standard cutoff, 84% were correctly classified. For the SUB scale, using the standard cutoff, 74% of patients were correctly classified as having substance abuse problems. With a lower cutoff to counteract underreporting, 77% of patients were correctly classified. The authors concluded that evaluators can use the problem-specific scales for SUI and SUB with an adaptation for SUI and a lower cutoff for SUB.

In another line of research, Hall and colleagues (2013) studied the reliability and validity of the Beck Depression Inventory-II (BDI-II) in bariatric surgery candidates. Five hundred and five prospective bariatric surgery patients were administered the BDI-II, the PAI depression scale (which had already been shown to have adequate internal consistency in bariatric surgery patients), and a semistructured clinical interview to assess for symptoms of major depressive disorder. There were moderate to large correlations with the PAI depression scale and its three subscales, and patients clinically diagnosed with depression had significantly greater scores on the BDI-II and PAI and each of their subscales. The authors concluded that "the BDI-II is a useful assessment measure for depressive symptoms in candidates seeking bariatric surgery" (Hall et al., 2013, p. 298).

As can be seen in the brief review of tests named here, there are a number of challenges to developing or adapting psychological tests for use in presurgical psychological evaluations of bariatric surgery patients. As a group, bariatric surgery patients are likely to underreport some types of problems, such as substance abuse, because they want to be approved for surgery. They are also more likely than the general population to obtain high scores on some scales because high scores reflect problems that are related to obesity such as chronic health concerns. For these reasons, the tests used in presurgical evaluation of bariatric surgery patients have to be normed on prospective bariatric patients in order for results to be accurately interpreted. In addition, the tests have to be reliable and validated against meaningful external criteria.

A number of tests are available to measure eating behavior and screen for eating disorders, to measure quality of life, and to assess for specific problems including substance abuse. Marek et al. (2016) reviewed several measures for their suitability for presurgical evaluation of bariatric surgery patients, and they recommend specific instruments for assessing eating behaviors, substance use, and depression on the basis of their review.

JOANNE'S EXPERIENCE WITH PSYCHOLOGICAL TESTING PRIOR TO BARIATRIC SURGERY

Joanne met with Dr. Jiang for her presurgical mental health evaluation. Joanne was nervous about the meeting. She decided she wanted the surgery and didn't want anything to hold her back. Dr. Jiang asked Joanne a lot of questions about her background, including her history of mental health treatment, her current family and work situation, her use of drugs and alcohol, her eating habits, and her goals for the surgery. Dr. Jiang also explained how the surgery would go and what to expect afterward. She asked Joanne about the kinds of support she had at home and about her husband's willingness to make changes in their home life to support her in the coming year. She also gave Joanne a test, the MMPI-2-RF. Joanne took the test on a computer in Dr. Jiang's office. When she was done, the receptionist scheduled a return visit to go over the results.

At the return visit, Dr. Jiang discussed a few concerns that came up during the evaluation, including Joanne's history of recurrent depression and some problematic eating habits. Dr. Jiang and Joanne made a plan about how to manage these problems. Joanne did well with the surgery and continued to lose weight over the next year. Although she remained overweight, her health improved and she was better able to engage in physical activities. She felt better too.

CONCLUSION

Presurgical psychological, or mental health, evaluation is an important component of bariatric surgery, so much so that most insurance companies and surgical teams require it. The purpose is twofold: to identify problems that could interfere with recovery from surgery and make plans to manage them and to promote positive outcomes from surgery.

Although no standard battery of tests is recommended for presurgical psychological evaluation, symptom measures, personality measures, measures of eating habits and eating disorders, other measures of specific psychiatric or substance abuse problems, and quality of life measures have all been employed. Several factors are important to consider in choosing tests to use for presurgical evaluation. The test must have appropriate norms as bariatric surgery candidates want to be approved for surgery and are likely to underreport some types of problems. They are also likely to have certain kinds of problems, such as chronic health concerns, as a function of obesity, and these would be reflected in overly high scores on some scales relative to a nonobese population. In addition, the chosen tests must be shown to have reliability and to be valid for their intended purpose of screening for problems associated with poor surgical outcomes and promoting positive outcomes. Finally, using cutoff scores that apply to the general population could incorrectly identify problems in bariatric surgery candidates. The development of norms, tests, protocols, and cutoff scores for presurgical evaluation of bariatric surgery candidates continues to be an active area of research.

Discussion Questions

1. Should scores on psychological tests determine if a patient is permitted to undergo bariatric surgery? Why or why not?

2. How can psychological tests help patients who are planning to undergo bariatric surgery have a good outcome from surgery?

3. If you were a clinician, which tests, or which kinds of tests, would you use to evaluate patients prior to bariatric surgery, and why would you choose them?

Research Ideas

1. Conduct a literature review to find out how psychological testing is used for gender variant clients prior to medical interventions. Discuss issues and controversies that researchers and clinicians are grappling with and speculate on the future of psychological testing with this group of clients.

2. Discuss the use of the MMPI scales (MMPI, MMPI-2, MMPI-RF) and other psychological tests with chronic pain patients.

3. Review the literature on psychological testing in the assessment and treatment of eating disorders. Choose at least two tests and discuss the evidence for, or against, using each test in a medical setting.

References

American Society for Metabolic and Bariatric Surgery. (2017). *Who is a candidate for bariatric surgery?* Retrieved from http://asmbs.org/patients/who-is-a-candidate-for-bariatric-surgery

Bauchowitz, A. U., Gonder-Frederick, L. A., Olbrisch, M. E., Azarbad, L., Ryee, M. Y., Woodson, M., Miller, A., & Schirmer, B. (2005). Psychosocial evaluation of bariatric surgery candidates: A survey of present practices. *Psychosomatic Medicine, 67*, 825–832.

Centers for Disease Control and Prevention. (2017). *Adult obesity causes & consequences.* Retrieved from http://www.cdc.gov/obesity/adult/causes.html

Colligan, R. C., Rasmussen, N. H., Agerter, D. C., Offord, K. P., Malinchoc, M., O'Byrne, M. M., & Benson, J. T. (2008). The MMPI-2: A contemporary normative study of midwestern family medicine outpatients. *Journal of Clinical Psychology in Medical Settings, 15*(2), 98–119.

Fabricatore, A. N, Crerand, C. E., & Wadden, T. A., Sarwer, D. B., & Krasucki, J. L. (2013). How do mental health professionals evaluate candidates for bariatric surgery? Survey results. *Obesity Surgery, 16*(5), 567–573.

Hall, B. J., Hood, M. M., Nackers, L. M., Azarbad, L., Ivan, I., & Corsica, J. (2013, March). Confirmatory factor analysis of the Beck Depression Inventory-II in bariatric surgery candidates. *Psychological Assessment, 25*(1), 294–299. Retrieved from http://dx.doi.org/10.1037/a0030305

Heinberg, L. (2013, February 21). The role of psychological testing for bariatric/metabolic surgery candidates. *Bariatric Times*.

Marcus, M. D., Kalarchian, M. A., & Courcoulas, A. P. (2009). Psychiatric evaluation and follow-up of bariatric surgery patients. *American Journal of Psychiatry, 166*(3), 285–291.

Marek, R. J., Heinberg, L. J., Lavery, M., Rish, J. M., & Ashton, K. (2016). A review of psychological assessment instruments for use in bariatric surgery evaluations. *Psychological Assessment, 28*(9), 1142–1157.

Meana, M., & Ricciardi, L. (2008). *Obesity surgery: Stories of altered lives.* Reno: University of Nevada Press.

Mechanick, J. I., Youdim, A., Jones, D. B., Garvey, W. T., Hurley, D. L., McMahon, M. M., . . . Brethauer, S. (2013, March/April). Clinical practice guidelines for the perioperative nutritional metabolic and nonsurgical support of the bariatric surgery patient—2013 update. *Endocrine Practice, 19*(2), e1–e36.

National Guideline Clearinghouse. (2008, July–August). *Clinical practice guidelines for the perioperative nutritional, metabolic, and nonsurgical support of the bariatric surgery patient – 2013 update: cosponsored by American Association of Clinical Endocrinologists, The Obesity Society, and American Society for Metabolic and Bariatric Surgery.* Retrieved from https://www.guideline.gov/summaries/summary/ 47785/clinical-practice-guidelines-for-the-perioperative-nutritional-metabolic-and-nonsurgical-support-of-the-bariatric-surgery-patient-2013-update-cosponsored-by-american-association-of-clinical-endocrinologists-the-obesity-

society-and-american-society-for-metabol?q= bariatric+surgery

Ogden, C. L., Carroll, M. D., Fryar, C. D., & Flegal, K. M. (2015, November). *NCHS data brief: Prevalence of obesity among adults and youth: United States, 2011-2014* (No. 219). Bethesda, MD: National Center for Biotechnology Information, US National Library of Medicine.

Picot, J., Jones, J., Colquitt, J. L., Gospodarevskaya, E., Loveman, E., Baxter, L., & Clegg, A. J. (2009, September). The clinical effectiveness and cost-effectiveness of bariatric (weight loss) surgery for obesity: A systematic review and economic evaluation. *Health Technol Assess., 13*(41), 1–190, 215–357, iii–iv. doi: 10.3310/hta13410

Sarwer, D. B., Allison, K. C., Bailer, B., Faulconbridge, L. F., & Wadden, T. A. (2013). Bariatric surgery. In A. R. Block, & D. B. Sarwer (Eds.), *Presurgical psychological screening: Understanding patients, improving outcomes* (pp. 61–83). Washington, DC: American Psychological Association. Retrieved from http://dx.doi.org/10.1037/14035-004

Sogg, S., Lauretti, J., & West-Smith, L. (2016). *Recommendations for the presurgical psychosocial evaluation of bariatric surgery patients.* Retrieved from https://asmbs.org/wp/uploads/2016/06/2016-Psych-Guidelines-published.pdf

Tarescavage, A. M., Windover, A., Ben-Porath, Y. S., Boutacoff, L. I., Marek, R. J., Ashton, K., Heinberg, L. J. (2013, August). Use of the MMPI-2-RF Suicidal/death ideation and substance abuse scales in screening bariatric surgery candidates. *Psychological Assessment, 25*(4), 1384–1389. doi:10.1037/a0034045

Tarescavage, A. M., Wygant, D. B., Boutacoff, L. I., & Ben-Porath, Y. S. (2013, December). Reliability, validity, and utility of the Minnesota multiphasic personality inventory–2–restructured form (MMPI–2–RF) in assessments of bariatric surgery candidates. *Psychological Assessment, 25*(4), 1179–1194. doi:10.1037/a0033694

Wise, E. A., & Streiner, D. L. (2010). A comparison of the millon behavioral medical diagnostic and millon behavioral health inventory with medical populations. *Journal of Clinical Psychology, 66*(12), 1281–1291.

PSYCHOLOGICAL TESTING IN THE LEGAL ARENA

Child Custody in High Conflict Divorce

LEARNING OBJECTIVES

- Explain why psychological tests used in forensic settings require strong psychometric foundations

- Describe how forensic psychologists can show that the tests they used in a specific case were valid for the purpose they were intended to serve

- Identify the chief differences between a clinical and forensic evaluation

- Define Daubert criteria and explain how Daubert criteria are relevant to psychological testing in legal contexts

- Discuss the importance of considering the context of the evaluation when interpreting test findings in child custody disputes

- Explain why psychologists use both computer and evaluator generated interpretations of test results in child custody evaluations

Psychological tests are employed in many different legal contexts. A plaintiff in a civil suit alleging psychological harm, such as posttraumatic stress disorder or a traumatic brain injury, might be tested by a forensic psychologist to help determine the merits of the case. Psychological tests also might be employed in the evaluation of a criminal defendant who pleads not guilty by reason of insanity and in the evaluation of a teenager involved in the juvenile court to determine her treatment and rehabilitation needs. They can also contribute to determining whether a defendant is competent to stand trial.

In the forensic setting, that is, in settings that involve the law, it is imperative that psychological tests have strong psychometric foundations. The decisions that psychological tests contribute to in forensic settings can have a significant impact on individual liberties and the outcome of civil suits. In addition, in an adversarial climate, such as a legal dispute, attorneys on both sides very closely examine the evidence, including psychological tests that were used in the case and the findings resulting from them.

The forensic psychologist needs to provide strong evidence that the tests he or she is using are reliable and valid for the purpose they are intended to serve. In this chapter, the use of psychological tests in divorce-related child-custody disputes is examined to demonstrate some of the many challenges of employing psychological tests in legal decision making.

PSYCHOLOGICAL TESTING IN CHILD CUSTODY DISPUTES: MR. AND MRS. KELLY

When a couple with children divorce, they have to agree on financial issues, a parenting plan, and decision-making responsibility for their children. Most couples work out an agreement that is entered in court, but some couples cannot come to an agreement, even with the help of mediators or a collaborative divorce process. For couples in this situation, a judge might order a child custody evaluation by a mental health provider.

This is the case for Mr. and Mrs. Kelly (a fictitious couple). They are getting divorced after 10 years of marriage, and they are fighting bitterly over custody of their two children, a two-year-old girl and an eight-year-old boy. They worked with a mediator for more than a year and could not agree on a parenting plan. Mr. Kelly made allegations that Mrs. Kelly was a negligent parent. Mrs. Kelly made allegations that Mr. Kelly was emotionally abusive to the children. They each accused the other parent of saying terrible things to the children—specifically, terrible things about each other. The children still live in the family home with both parents, neither of whom will move out for fear of losing the home and custody of the children.

Neither of the children are doing well. The two-year-old, Jessica, is clingy, has frequent tantrums, and is not adding to her meager vocabulary. The eight-year-old, Sean, gets into fights with other children at school, and nobody invites him to playdates or birthday parties. He is having problems with reading and math, and his grades and test scores are poor.

The family law judge ordered Mr. and Mrs. Kelly to undergo a child custody evaluation with Dr. Lissette, a psychologist who specializes in child custody evaluations in high-conflict divorce. Child custody disputes that are so extreme that they are decided in court are extremely complex and contentious, and psychologists who conduct evaluations related to child custody disputes must have special expertise. Ideally, as in the Kelly case, the child custody evaluator is a neutral party appointed by the court. Mr. and Mrs. Kelly reluctantly agreed to the evaluation, splitting Dr. Lissette's very high fee.

Child custody evaluations are ordered by family law judges in a small subset of high-conflict divorce cases, those in which parents cannot agree on custody issues and parenting plans. Specific decisions need to be made on where the child will live (physical custody), when and where the child will see each parent (parenting time), who can make decisions about the child (legal custody), and child support (financial support of the child).

How can Dr. Lissette help the court determine a parenting plan for this family? In every state, the current standard for making decisions about child custody issues, including parenting time and other matters, is to develop a plan based on *the best interests of the child*. There are no general standards that define the best interests of the child, although some states identify factors that should be considered in making the determination (Zumbach & Koglin, 2015).

Couples in such high conflict that they can't agree on a parenting plan are challenging for psychologists tasked with evaluating them. Each parent is heavily invested in his or her own point of view and believes strongly in the rightness of his or her cause. Mr. Kelly knows *for sure* that Mrs. Kelly is a terrible parent who will put their children at risk of harm. Mrs. Kelly knows *for sure* that Mr. Kelly is a terrible parent who does emotional damage to their children every day. There may be significant financial ramifications as well. Both parents will do everything they can to maintain custody and decision-making ability, and neither can afford to be open and honest about their own parenting challenges, if they are even aware of them.

Dr. Lissette knows all about these kinds of couples. He has years of experience. He also relies on guidelines for child custody evaluation put forward by the American Psychological Association (APA) and Association of Family and Conciliation Courts (AFCC). To conduct the evaluation, he gathers information about each member of the family. He contacts the children's pediatrician and teachers and observes the children with each parent separately, once at home and once at his office. He interviews both parents using a semistructured interview format, and he carefully records their responses and his observations. He administers the Minnesota Multiphasic Personality Inventory-2 (MMPI-2) and the Rorschach Inkblot Method to both parents, and he has them complete the Child Behavior Checklist (CBCL) for the children. He is cautious in his interpretation of test results, paying attention to the normative data for child custody litigants and related problems with defensive responding. He compiles the data from interviews, observations, and testing, and he prepares a comprehensive report that describes the strengths and weaknesses of each parent, the children's needs, and how the children's best interests fit with the parent characteristics he identified. Then he prepares to testify in court, knowing that attorneys for one or both parents will question his findings.

A BRIEF HISTORY OF CHILD CUSTODY EVALUATION

In early American history, children were economic assets in a family, and custody was always given to the father as head of the household. As families moved away from farms, mothers were given preference in custody disputes unless they were deemed unfit, under the belief that mothers were better and more natural caretakers, especially for young children. This changed in the last half of the 20th century, when courts determined that mothers were not necessarily better qualified to provide care than fathers, and the notion that custody decisions should be made on the basis of the best interests of the child, rather than on meeting the needs of either parent, became part of the legal code in most states. This has remained the rule for the past several years, despite a lack of clarity about how to determine a child's best interests.

Child custody evaluation in divorce cases began in earnest in the 1970s, following legislation that allowed courts to order professional consultation for custody matters. The role of custody evaluators has been controversial ever since, and child custody evaluation has also been fraught with ethical challenges. What should an evaluator who is trying to be impartial do if one parent refuses to be evaluated? What kinds of recommendations should be made if research does not support one decision or another regarding child custody and visitation? What are reasonable methods to obtain data? These kinds of ethical concerns were noted 30 years ago (see Karras & Berry, 1985) and continue to be relevant. Questions about the evaluator's decision-making process, the kinds of custody arrangements that are feasible and helpful to children, and many other matters have also been posed for years. The answers to these questions initially tended to be based on opinions, with little research support to back them up (Keilin & Bloom, 1986). To some extent, that is still the case.

The APA came out with its first set of guidelines for child custody evaluation in 1994. The guidelines reference concerns about the misuse of psychologists' expertise in some child custody cases, and they provide direction to evaluators in order to enhance their proficiency and minimize the likelihood of ethical lapses. The 1994 guidelines indicate, for example, that the psychologist should develop specialized competence, strive to maintain impartiality, and make custody recommendations that are in the best interest of the child, focusing on the fit between the needs of the child and parenting capacities. The guidelines were revised in 2010, and they are discussed below.

THE FORENSIC NATURE OF CHILD CUSTODY EVALUATIONS

Much of the time, psychologists conduct evaluations to help individuals. In the case of child custody evaluations, the role of the evaluator is to help the court make decisions about custody of one or more children in a family. The client is the court. Forensic evaluations provide guidance to court personnel on both civil and criminal matters. They require a higher standard of evidence than clinical evaluations because the stakes are so high and the process is adversarial. If the evaluator does not support his or her findings with strong evidence based on scientific research, the findings can be dismissed.

In forensic work, there are two standards for admissibility of evidence in court. Daubert criteria for admissibility of evidence stem from a 1993 case, *Daubert v. Merrell Dow Pharmaceuticals,* that was decided by the Supreme Court. In that case, the Court decided that expert witnesses must provide evidence based on a reliable foundation, that is, the expert's conclusions must be based on adequate scientific methodology. Furthermore, the judge in the case must serve as a gatekeeper in determining whether expert testimony is based on scientific knowledge. The judge evaluates the validity of the science in special hearings (Chin, 2014).

Daubert criteria are required in federal courts, but some states have not adopted the Daubert criteria for admissibility of evidence and rely on an earlier standard for admissibility, the Frye standard. The Frye standard requires that the scientific procedures relied on for providing evidence are generally accepted by the scientific community. Thus, for states relying on the Frye standard, it is the scientific community that is the gatekeeper, not the judge (Ackerman & Gould, 2015). In either case, testimony of expert witnesses is not admissible if it is based on clinical opinion rather than scientific evidence. As Ackerman and Gould (2015) state, "Expert testimony can no longer be admissible when the opinions are based on the clinical experience or intuition of the witness. Expert testimony must have its basis in peer-reviewed literature and/or data that have been drawn from scientific methods" (p. 431).

Thus, the evaluator serving as an expert witness must ensure that the evidence he or she provides is derived from sound science, or to meet the requirements of the Frye standard, derived from procedures generally accepted by the scientific community. In other words, to present evidence as an expert witness, the evaluator must use credible scientific techniques to gather information.

In addition, in child custody evaluations and other forensic work, the process is adversarial. The evaluator must be unbiased and make every effort to evaluate both parties in the dispute. Ideally, the evaluator is appointed by the court rather than hired by one of the parties.

The evaluator in a child custody case and in other forensic contexts serves as an *expert witness.* He or she provides information that others don't have, by virtue of his or her special expertise in the area in question. A child's psychotherapist, in contrast, can serve as a fact witness but not an expert witness in a custody case. The therapist as fact witness describes events and observations. It is very important that the roles of an expert witness and a fact witness not be confused. A therapist may have an opinion about a parenting plan, even a very strong opinion, but he or she was not hired or appointed by anyone to make recommendations, or provide findings, regarding custody issues. The therapist was hired to provide treatment. Furthermore, the therapist is not likely to be objective and unbiased.

Should the evaluator offer a recommendation about custody at the conclusion of the evaluation? This is an ongoing controversy among psychologists. Some psychologists provide information so the court can make informed decisions, while other psychologists make specific recommendations about custody and other aspects of parenting plans. Many psychologists are concerned that the scientific basis for making specific recommendations regarding parenting plans is inadequate (Symons, 2010).

As noted above, APA established guidelines for child custody evaluations in 1994, and these were revised in 2010. The purpose of the guidelines is to "promote proficiency" in child custody evaluation; the guidelines are aspirational (APA, 2010, p. 836). They do not set standards or mandate activities.

According to APA guidelines, the psychologist's job is to "identify the psychological best interests of the child" taking into account a variety of factors, such as family dynamics, strengths and weaknesses of all parties, the child's needs, and cultural and environmental issues (2010, p. 864). The court uses this information in making decisions about child custody. The guidelines do not go as far as advising psychologists not to make specific recommendations about a parenting plan, but they advise that if the psychologist chooses to make recommendations they must be based on sound data.

The guidelines also recommend that the focus of the evaluation is on the child's needs, not the parents' needs, throughout the evaluation. Specifically, the guidelines recommend that the evaluation focuses on the child's needs, parent characteristics, and the fit between them based on scientifically reliable information. They further advise evaluators to use multiple methods of gathering information.

In addition to APA guidelines, Ackerman and Gould (2015) list 24 current standards and guidelines for child custody evaluations, noting first that child custody evaluations are forensic evaluations.

THE PROCESS OF CHILD CUSTODY EVALUATIONS

Dr. Lissette is the right person for the job of identifying the psychological best interests of the Kelly children and how to meet them. He is very familiar with child custody evaluation and has served as an expert witness in similar cases several times. He is knowledgeable about child development, family dynamics, the impact of divorce and separation on children, psychopathology, assessment in custody cases, and legal proceedings in divorce for his state. He has kept up with research in the area and revised his procedures over the years to provide the most scientifically sound findings. He is well versed in the ethics of assessment in child custody cases, the need to remain unbiased, and the importance of carefully obtaining informed consent. He is skilled at writing a report to document his findings, and he is well prepared to testify in court as an expert witness. He will not be providing a recommendation about custody, a decision he made recently, because he does not want to state more than the science will support.

Most of his clinical time with the members of the Kelly family is taken up by interviews and observations, both of which he carefully documents. He also obtains collateral information, such as reports from school and the pediatrician, and statements from Mr. Kelly, Mrs. Kelly, Mrs. Kelly's therapists, and a marriage counselor who worked with them briefly.

Then he administers psychological tests. The purpose of the tests, in his view, is to generate hypotheses about Mr. and Mrs. Kelly's parenting strengths and weaknesses that can be borne out by interview and other data. Rather than providing a generalized assessment, he focuses on Mr. and Mrs. Kelly's capacities to parent and to coparent, that is, to work together as parents in the best interest of the children. He is specifically looking for signs of mental health problems, substance abuse, and/or cognitive and learning deficits that could interfere with parenting or coparenting, and he is also interested in learning more about their personality characteristics, for the same reason. His goal is to inform the court about strengths and challenges in these areas for each parent.

He knows that Mr. and Mrs. Kelly are likely to respond to psychological tests defensively, given the context of the evaluation and their need to be seen in a favorable light. He therefore uses tests that have both standard normative data and normative data from child custody litigants, in order to make the most informed interpretations of test data. He uses computer generated reports as well as his own interpretations of the data. The computer generated reports are less susceptible to bias, but he cannot access the algorithms behind the reports because they are proprietary and therefore he cannot readily defend them in court.

He also asks the court to order an evaluation of the older child, to be completed by a psychologist who has expertise in evaluating young children with learning and emotional problems. He could not determine from the available data, including evaluations completed at school, whether Sean had a learning disability or emotional problems or whether his challenges were due to the stress of his family situation. He wanted to understand Sean's needs so he could factor them into his findings about parenting capacities. He relied on pediatrician reports and developmental testing completed by the pediatrician's office to understand the younger child's needs.

After he gathers all of the data, Dr. Lissette writes a comprehensive report that outlines his findings. He focuses on parenting strengths and weaknesses as well as how to improve each parent's ability to coparent and each parent's effectiveness with the children. He focuses on both parenting and coparenting because he knows that the children will do best if they have strong relationships with each parent and if their parents can work together on childrearing with minimal conflict. This is what he is hoping for the Kelly family.

PSYCHOLOGICAL TESTS USED IN CUSTODY EVALUATION

The most important consideration in choosing psychological tests to use in custody evaluations is to ensure that the tests have strong research support. Each test must have strong evidence of reliability and validity in regard to the specific questions under consideration (Ackerman & Gould, 2015). The tests should also have separate normative data for male and female custody litigants (Ackerman & Gould, 2015) because of the special nature of the context of the evaluation. If the evaluator uses tests that have inadequate research support, his or her findings could be contested by one of the parent's attorneys. Equally important, if he or she relies on unreliable data or data that lacks validity in determining parenting strengths and weaknesses, the evaluation would be grossly unjust to the children, whose needs are not being met, and to the parent on the losing end of the custody battle.

Another important issue in choosing and using psychological tests in custody disputes is that the context of the evaluation needs to be factored in when interpreting results. Custody disputes are extraordinarily stressful, and the level of stress custody litigants are under can impact test results. Anger about being evaluated can also impact results. Thus, the custody litigant is more distressed than he or she would be otherwise and may seem more maladjusted. Most common, however, is that custody litigants respond to psychological tests in a very defensive manner, portraying themselves in as favorable light as possible. They may even be coached to do so by their attorney (see Victor & Abeles, 2004). Paying attention to the context can mitigate the effect of either of these problems in test interpretation.

In choosing tests, the primary goal is to measure attributes that are relevant to the specific questions posed by the court, and, more generally, to measure attributes that are relevant to parenting effectiveness. Parents who have untreated mental illness, substance abuse, or neuropsychological deficits that may affect impulse control and judgment can engage in poor or even destructive parenting practices. Another goal for evaluation might be to assess personality and coping characteristics that can interfere with, or support, coparenting. Psychological tests can be used to generate hypotheses in all of these areas. Hypotheses are then substantiated, or not, by interview, observational, and collateral data. Tests add an important layer of data, one that is objective and standardized, but they are not the final word.

No psychological test is perfect for use in custody disputes. The MMPI-2 comes closest and is considered the "gold standard" (Ackerman & Gould, 2015, p. 436; King, 2013). The MMPI-2 has a tremendous amount of research behind it and includes scales that measure defensive responding. In addition, MMPI-2 norms for custody litigants were first published in 1997 (King, 2013). Most custody litigants underreported negative attributes and overreported attributes that made them look good, understandable given that the test was administered to determine if the test taker should be awarded custody of his or her children. The custody litigants as a group looked psychologically healthier than the normal population based on MMPI-2 results, due to defensive responding (Bathurst, Gottfried, & Gottfried, 1997). Some evaluators manage the defensive responding of custody litigants by making corrections or adjustments to how the test results are usually interpreted, but the research does not yet support these efforts (King, 2013). Other evaluators might use elevated scores, rare in the custody litigant population, to generate hypotheses about problems one of the parents might have, such as antisocial behaviors. They don't make too much of scores in the normal range, other than to note that they are typical of custody litigants and likely reflect defensive responding that is appropriate to the context.

The newest version of the MMPI, the MMPI-2 RF, is less widely used than the MMPI-2 in custody evaluations because the data collected on the MMPI-2 does not generalize to the MMPI-2 RF, and there is less research on the newer test. There are other specific weaknesses of the test for assessing custody litigants, such as a lack of separate norms for men and women (King, 2013).

The Rorschach Inkblot Method, a projective test, is more controversial among psychologists than the MMPI-2, but there is good evidence for its utility in measuring psychosis and related signs of serious psychopathology (Mihura, Meyer, Dumitrascu, & Bombel, 2013), and it is not infrequently used in custody evaluations (King, 2013).

Standard measures of cognitive functioning, such as the Wechsler Adult Intelligence Scales-IV (WAIS-IV), can be useful in situations where there are questions about cognitive functioning for one or both parents. These kinds of tests are not prone to defensive responding, but results can be impacted to a mild degree by anxiety, and that should be taken into account given the assessment context. Similarly, measures of academic achievement such as the Woodcock Johnson Tests of Achievement-IV (WJA-IV) can be helpful in ruling out learning disabilities. Tests of cognitive functioning and academic achievement should be considered methods of learning what parents need to do their job effectively, to help develop a parenting plan that is in the best interest of the child, rather than as a means of determining who should have custody.

Use of both computer and evaluator-generated interpretations for all tests are recommended, computer interpretation because of its thoroughness, grounding in research findings, and lack of bias, and evaluator-generated interpretation because computer interpretation is based on algorithms that are proprietary and therefore cannot be readily defended in court.

In addition to psychological tests to make hypotheses about parent functioning, it can be helpful to have parents complete rating scales about the behavior of their children. There are several very well researched measures, such as the Achenbach Child Behavior Checklist (CBCL) or the Behavior Assessment System for Children (BASC), although there are no specific norms for children whose parents are in a custody dispute about them. These kinds of tests can be useful in gaining insight into each parent's view about a child's behavior, especially when examined in comparison to other data about the child.

Although there are a few measures of parent effectiveness, most are not well validated or have limited normative data. The Parenting Stress Index (PSI), a self-report measure of stress in parenting, is a useful test in some circumstances, but it has limited normative data and is prone to defensive responding in custody litigants (King, 2013). There are also some measures that have been developed specifically for use in custody litigation, such as the Bricklin Perceptual Scales, but none of these have adequate research support.

HOW DO PSYCHOLOGICAL TESTS CONTRIBUTE TO DR. LISSETTE'S OPINION ABOUT WHAT IS IN THE BEST INTEREST OF THE KELLY CHILDREN?

For the Kelly family, psychological testing of the parents using the MMPI-2 and the Rorschach provided Dr. Lissette with hypotheses about each parent's personality characteristics, parenting strengths, and parenting limitations. Both parents responded to the MMPI-2 defensively, in a manner typical of custody litigants, and all scores were in the normal range. They also responded to the Rorschach defensively, providing a minimal number of responses but enough to score the test in accordance with Exner scoring criteria (Exner, 1986). Rorschach results suggested each parent had limitations in coping skills, with Mr. Kelly likely to have temper outbursts when stressed and Mrs. Kelly likely to have mild perceptual distortions, seeing the world other than as it is in stressful circumstances. Dr. Lissette's observations and interviews with Mr. and Mrs. Kelly and their marriage counselor supported these notions. Both parents would be more effective if they had mental health counseling to improve their coping and parenting skills as well as their capacity to coparent.

CBCL results suggested Mrs. Kelly minimized Sean's behavior and learning problems, while Mr. Kelly tended to exaggerate them. They both would benefit from education about child development and consultation with a counselor and the school psychologist to more accurately understand Sean's needs. Results of Sean's testing, completed by a different evaluator, indicated he had a reading disorder in addition to emotional problems related to the stress of the divorce. As a result, he would need to be monitored for an individualized education plan and special education services as he got older. He would also need more immediate help at school to improve his reading skills and capacity to pay attention during the school day.

Dr. Lissette included the test findings and his interpretations in the comprehensive report he made to the court. When he took the stand as an expert witness, attorneys on both sides asked questions about the tests he administered and the findings they generated. Dr. Lissette was able to respond to them easily. All of the tests he used have strong scientific support and meet both Daubert and Frye criteria for admissibility in child custody cases. He is well qualified to conduct child custody evaluations. His interpretations of test results served as hypotheses rather than conclusions. They were based on normative data from custody litigants as well as a normal population, and his findings were based on computer-generated interpretations as well as his own interpretations of the data. He took into account the likelihood of defensive responding and the stressful nature of the circumstances for the parents and children. He focused on identifying the psychological best interests of the children and both parents' capacities to meet them. He made recommendations about how to improve the capacities of the parents to meet their children's needs, but he refrained from making a parenting plan for the family, leaving that to the court.

CONCLUSION

Psychological tests play a role in most court-ordered child custody evaluations. They provide objective, standardized data in a complex, adversarial situation. When used wisely, by a psychologist with expertise in the area and as part of a more comprehensive assessment to address specific concerns, psychological tests provide important hypotheses that can be substantiated through historical records, interviews, and observations. It is essential that the tests used in these matters have strong psychometric foundations. If not, they will not only be contested in court, they can provide misleading data to guide very important legal decisions, an unjust outcome for all concerned.

Discussion Questions

1. Should child custody evaluations conclude with recommendations about the specifics of parenting plans, such as how much time children should spend with each parent and how holidays should be handled? Why or why not?

2. If you were an evaluator in a custody dispute, how would you decide which tests to administer?

3. What do you think were the challenges for Dr. Lissette in the case described above?

Research Ideas

1. Review the literature on at least two measures that are used to assess the risk for future violence, such as the Structured Assessment for Violence Risk in Youth (SAVRY) and the Psychopathy Checklist-Revised (PCL-R). How were these tests developed, when is it appropriate to use them, and what is the evidence that supports their use?

2. Discuss the use of psychological testing in determining competency to stand trial.

3. Review the literature on the assessment of malingering, or the exaggeration or faking of illness for secondary gain, for example, to claim disability or to avoid legal or other consequences. Are there tests that are successful at identifying malingering? What is the evidence for or against their effectiveness?

References

Ackerman, M. J., & Gould, J. W. (2015). Child custody and access. In B. L. Cutler, & P. A. Zapf (Eds.), *APA handbooks in psychology. APA handbook of forensic psychology, Vol. 1. Individual and situational influences in criminal and civil contexts* (pp. 425–469). Retrieved from http://dx.doi.org/10.1037/14461-013

American Psychological Association. (1994, July). Guidelines for child custody evaluations in divorce proceedings. *American Psychologist, 49*(7), 677–680.

American Psychological Association. (2010, December). Guidelines for child custody evaluations in family law proceedings. *American Psychologist, 65*(9), 863–867. Retrieved from http://dx.doi.org/10.1037/a0021250

Bathurst, K., Gottfried, A. W., & Gottfried, A. E. (1997). Normative data for the MMPI-2 in child custody litigation. *Psychological Assessment, 9*(3), 205–211. doi:10.1037/1040-3590.9.3.205

Chin, J. M. (2014, August). Psychological sciences replicability crisis and what it means for science in the courtroom. *Psychology, Public Policy, and Law, 20*(3), 225–238.

Exner, J. E., Jr. (1986). *The Rorschach: A comprehensive system* (2nd ed.). New York, NY: Wiley.

Karras, D., & Berry, K. K. (1985, February). Custody evaluations: A critical review. *Professional Psychology: Research and Practice, 16*(1), 76–85.

Keilin, W. G., & Bloom, L. J. (1986). Child custody evaluation practices: A survey of experienced professionals. *Professional Psychology: Research and Practice, 17*(4), 338–346.

King, H. E. (2013). Assessment in custody hearings: Child custody evaluations. In K. F. Geisinger, B. A. Bracken, J. F. Carlson, J.-I. C. Hansen, N. R. Kuncel, S. P. Reise, & M. C. Rodriguez (Eds.), *APA handbooks in psychology. APA handbook of testing and assessment in psychology, Vol. 2. Testing and assessment in clinical and counseling psychology* (pp. 587-605). Washington, DC: American Psychological Association. Retrieved from http://dx.doi.org/10.1037/14048-034

Mihura, J. L., Meyer, G. J., Dumitrascu, N., & Bombel, G. (2013, May). The validity of individual Rorschach variables: Systematic reviews and meta-analyses of the comprehensive system. *Psychological Bulletin, 139*(3), 548–605. doi:10.1037/a0029406

Symons, D. K. (2010, June). A review of the practice and science of child custody and access assessment in the United States and Canada. *Professional Psychology: Research and Practice, 41*(3), 267–273. Retrieved from http://dx.doi.org/10.1037/a0019271

Victor, T. L., & Abeles, N. (2004, August). Coaching clients to take psychological and neuropsychological tests: A clash of ethical obligations. *Professional Psychology: Research and Practice, 35*(4), 373–379. Retrieved from http://dx.doi.org/10.1037/0735-7028.35.4.373

Zumbach, J., & Koglin, U. (2015). Psychological evaluations in family law proceedings: A systematic review of the contemporary literature. *Professional Psychology: Research and Practice, 46*(4), 221–234. Retrieved from http://dx.doi.org/10.1037/a0039329

PSYCHOLOGICAL TESTING IN DETERMINING DISABILITY

Intellectual Disability and the Death Penalty

LEARNING OBJECTIVES

- Describe how intellectual disability is defined and who is responsible for defining it
- Discuss how psychological testing is used in identifying intellectual disability
- Explain the concept of normal distribution of intelligence and how it applies to intelligence testing
- Explain how measurement error is accounted for in testing for intellectual disability
- Describe how adaptive functioning is measured
- Identify the problems in measurement of intellectual functioning associated with practice effects

Randi, a fictitious 35-year-old female, is on death row in Texas. She has a long history of learning problems, and her lawyers claim that she is intellectually disabled and therefore exempt from the death penalty. They arranged for her to be evaluated by a forensic psychologist, and the psychologist found that Randi's IQ was 69, in the range of mild intellectual disability. Her level of adaptive functioning was less clear because she was in prison and not much was expected of her. However, her family reported that she was slow to develop speech, she always had difficulty communicating with others, and she received special education services since early elementary school. She could read and write but not very skillfully. The psychologist determined that Randi likely had deficits in adaptive functioning and that a diagnosis of intellectual disability was warranted. Randi was also evaluated by a psychologist for the state, and he found she had low intellectual functioning but did not meet diagnostic criteria for intellectual disability. She obtained an IQ score of 71 and she seemed to function much like other inmates, without needing any special help. Her case is going to be heard soon, and it is not clear what the court will decide.

Randi's case is an extreme example of a much more ordinary concern, how to determine if someone has a disability. The determination is very important from a legal perspective because individuals who have disabilities are protected by the Americans with Disabilities Act (ADA). The legal definition of *disability* is a physical or mental impairment that substantially limits a major life activity. Psychological tests are sometimes used to document a disability because when scores are significantly below average, it is an indication that a person's ability to complete a related task is likely to be impaired. Just like for Randi, however, the determination of disability needs to go beyond test scores and include the impact of the impairment on everyday functioning.

INTELLECTUAL DISABILITY AND CAPITAL PUNISHMENT: A BRIEF HISTORY

The Eighth Amendment of the United States Constitution was written in the late 1700s and is part of the Bill of Rights. It outlaws cruel and unusual punishment. In 2002, as a result of a Supreme Court decision, the execution of defendants with intellectual disabilities became unlawful on the basis of the Eighth Amendment. Although the Supreme Court made it unlawful to execute individuals with intellectual disabilities, it left it up to individual states to define intellectual disability and to establish criteria and procedures for establishing whether an individual has an intellectual disability. Most states, if not all, rely on mental health professionals, typically psychologists or psychiatrists, to determine whether a defendant meets criteria for a diagnosis of intellectual disability, and mental health professionals rely on test scores to establish the diagnosis.

The definition of intellectual disability, criteria for the diagnosis, and procedures for establishing the diagnosis vary across states, and the criteria set by states are often different than medically established criteria for the diagnosis of intellectual disability. An individual might be correctly diagnosed with an intellectual disability using the criteria established by the American Psychiatric Association and codified in the *Diagnostic and Statistical Manual* but fail to meet criteria established by the state for the same purpose. Since the consequences of having an intellectual disability are so high for a defendant on death row, establishing whether a defendant meets the state's criteria for intellectual disability is extraordinarily important and often hard fought by both the defense and prosecutor. There may be several experts testifying on both sides of the case.

In 2013, Freddie Lee Hall challenged his death penalty sentence before the Supreme Court. The issue before the court was whether it is constitutional for a state to use a fixed IQ score to determine whether a defendant is intellectually disabled and therefore exempt from the death penalty (*Hall v. Florida, 2012*). Mr. Hall had an IQ score of 71, and Florida required defendants to have an IQ score of ≤ 70 to be diagnosed with an intellectual disability. In the Supreme Court's ruling, set down in 2014, it is unconstitutional for a state to use a fixed IQ score. Mr. Hall was spared from execution.

Warren Hill, a defendant in Georgia, petitioned the Supreme Court to reverse the death penalty in his case the previous year, 2012. The state of Georgia requires a defendant to prove beyond a reasonable doubt that he or she is intellectually disabled to avoid execution, a different criteria than that established in Florida. However, several mental health clinicians agreed that Mr. Hill was intellectually disabled based on a "preponderance of the evidence," this fell short of the requirement that his intellectual disability be proven "beyond a reasonable doubt," a stricter standard. The Supreme Court declined to hear his case, and Warren Hill was executed in Georgia in January of 2015.

Prior to 2002, it was not unconstitutional to execute individuals with intellectual disabilities. In fact, in 1989, in *Penry v. Lynaugh*, the Supreme Court specifically ruled that execution of intellectually disabled individuals did not violate the Eighth Amendment. Thirteen years later, in *Atkins v. Virginia*, the Court decided otherwise, due to evolving standards of decency in the nation and changes in the point of view of state legislatures. The state of Georgia outlawed the execution of intellectually disabled people in 1986. Other states followed between 1989 and 2002, and by the time the Atkins case came before the Court, most states that allowed the death penalty did not allow it for individuals with intellectual disabilities.

This chapter considers the scientific issues relevant to the diagnosis of intellectual disability and the implications for public policy. In the case of Freddie Lee Hall, evaluation of intellectual disability was a matter of life and death. Diagnosing an individual with intellectual disability typically has milder, but still very important, ramifications. For example, individuals with intellectual disabilities are often eligible for financial support through the Social Security Administration and eligible for independent living, social, and vocational support through state agencies. Individuals who don't meet state established criteria for the diagnosis of intellectual disability (or for the purpose of obtaining Social Security benefits, criteria established by the Social Security Administration) may not be eligible for services even if they demonstrate a need for them.

WHY DOES THE DEATH PENALTY VIOLATE THE EIGHTH AMENDMENT FOR DEFENDANTS WITH INTELLECTUAL DISABILITIES?

The death penalty is highly controversial. Although it is lawful under the constitution, that has not always been the case. As of this writing, the death penalty is permitted in 32 states and by the federal government, a number that has been in decline in recent years. In 2013, 39 inmates were executed (see www.bjs.gov for additional statistics). At the end of 2013, close to 3,000 inmates were in prison and sentenced to death in the United States. A small percentage have or might have an intellectual disability.

The constitution as interpreted by the Supreme Court permits the death penalty in a narrow range of circumstances. In any other circumstances, the death penalty violates the Eighth Amendment of the Constitution, the part of the Bill of Rights that bans cruel and unusual punishment.

The death penalty is reserved for the *worst of the worst* crimes. The crime must be so bad that it deserves the most extreme form of punishment. A case before the court in 1972, *Furman v. Georgia*, found that the death penalty could not be applied arbitrarily, to one person and not another who was convicted of a similar crime. Later cases before the Supreme Court found that the death penalty could only be applied for certain crimes or when there were aggravating circumstances, such as lack of remorse or prior convictions. In addition, a defendant could avoid the death penalty when it would otherwise apply if there were mitigating circumstances, such as a history of abuse.

Individuals who have intellectual disabilities are exempted from the death penalty because their limitations make them less culpable than those without limitations; they cannot be the worst of the worst. The intellectually disabled have a lower capacity for regulating their behavior than those without disabilities, and they have poorer capacities for decision making and moral reasoning. They also can't understand legal concepts as well as others, they are more vulnerable to outside pressures, and they are not as effective in assisting in their own defense (Haney, Weill, & Lynch, 2015). Juveniles and those defendants with mitigating factors, such as an abusive background, are exempt from the death penalty for similar reasons. The imposition of the death penalty is also not thought to be a deterrent to individuals with intellectual disabilities because they are less able to learn and make rational decisions based on abstract information.

DEFINING INTELLECTUAL DISABILITY

Intellectual disability is defined by three important entities, the American Association for Intellectual and Developmental Disabilities (AAIDD), the American Psychiatric Association (APA), and the Social Security Administration (SSA).

From the AAIDD (2017):

Intellectual disability is a disability characterized by significant limitations in both **intellectual functioning** and in **adaptive behavior**, which covers many everyday social and practical skills. This disability originates **before the age of 18**.

Intellectual functioning—also called intelligence—refers to general mental capacity, such as learning, reasoning, problem solving, and so on. One way to measure intellectual functioning is an IQ test. Generally, an IQ test score of around 70 or as high as 75 indicates a limitation in intellectual functioning. (para 1)

Adaptive behavior is the collection of conceptual, social, and practical skills that are learned and performed by people in their everyday lives.

Conceptual skills—language and literacy; money, time, and number concepts; and self-direction.

Social skills—interpersonal skills, social responsibility, self-esteem, gullibility, naïveté (i.e., wariness), social problem solving, and the ability to follow rules/obey laws and to avoid being victimized.

Practical skills—activities of daily living (personal care), occupational skills, healthcare, travel/transportation, schedules/routines, safety, use of money, use of the telephone. (para 4)

Standardized tests can also determine limitations in adaptive behavior. (para 5)

This condition is one of several developmental disabilities—that is, there is evidence of the disability during the developmental period, which in the US is operationalized as before the age of 18. (para 6)

The APA provides diagnostic criteria for intellectual disability in the *Diagnostic and Statistical Manual* (APA, 2013), as follows:

Intellectual disability

Deficits in intellectual functions, such as reasoning, problem solving, planning, abstract thinking, judgment, academic learning, and learning from experience, confirmed by both clinical assessment and individualized, standardized intelligence testing.

Deficits in adaptive functioning that result in failure to meet developmental and sociocultural standards for personal independence and social responsibility. Without ongoing support, the adaptive deficits limit functioning in one or more activities of daily life, such as communication, social participation, and independent living, across multiple environments, such as home, school, work, and community.

Onset of intellectual and adaptive deficits during the developmental period. (p. 33)

The Social Security Administration's definition of intellectual disability, or in their nomenclature, intellectual disorder, was recently revised. An individual applying for disability benefits on the basis of having an intellectual disorder, or claimant, must show "significantly subaverage general intellectual functioning; significant deficits in current adaptive functioning; and (that) the disorder manifested before age 22" (Social Security Administration, n.d., para 14). The determination of intellectual disorder for the Social Security Administration follows precise rules, depending on the level of cognitive inability. Claimants who are so cognitively disabled that they are unable to participate in standardized testing must show that they are dependent on caregivers for personal needs such as bathing. Individuals who are able to participate in testing must have a Full Scale IQ of 70 or below or a Full Scale IQ between 71–75 and a Performance or Verbal IQ below 70 on a standardized test of intellectual functioning. In addition, claimants must show

> Significant deficits in adaptive functioning currently manifested by extreme limitation of one, or marked limitation of two, of the following areas of mental functioning:
>
> A. Understand, remember, or apply information (see 12.00E1); or
>
> B. Interact with others (see 12.00E2); or
>
> C. Concentrate, persist, or maintain pace (see 12.00E3); or
>
> D. Adapt or manage oneself (see 12.00E4);
>
> E. For all individuals, the condition must have manifested prior to age 22.

LABELING AND DESCRIBING INTELLECTUAL DISABILITIES

The labels for intellectual disability change over time, most recently from mental retardation to intellectual disability, which is less stigmatizing and reflects current usage by professional associations, including the American Psychiatric Association (APA), the American Psychological Association (APA), and the American Association for Intellectual and Developmental Disabilities (AAIDD), formerly known as the American Association for Mental Retardation (AAMR). In addition, labels for the severity of an intellectual disability are applied based on the individual's level of intellectual and adaptive functioning. Individuals with moderate or severe intellectual disability are not able to function without a lot of assistance. There would not typically be a question of their culpability for a crime.

Individuals who have mild intellectual disability, especially those with IQ scores at the upper ends of the IQ range used to establish the diagnosis (those with IQs close to 70), are often able to function independently and might have basic academic and work skills. They might live on their own in the community and have a spouse and children. However, they learn more slowly and with more repetition than others, even if the material is simple and concrete, and they will be unable to grasp complex material or abstract concepts.

DIAGNOSING INTELLECTUAL DISABILITY: IQ TESTING

As is evident in the above definitions, no matter who sets the criteria or what the criteria are, determining if someone is intellectually disabled requires evidence of limitations in intellectual functioning, typically based on individual administration of a test of intellectual functioning, an IQ test. There are several options, but the Wechsler tests are widely used measures of intellectual functioning for children and adults. Other tests of intellectual functioning include the Stanford-Binet Intelligence Scales (SB5), the Kaufman Assessment Battery (KABC-II), and the Woodcock Johnson Tests of Cognitive Ability (W-J III NU Complete). The Wechsler scales, the Wechsler Intelligence Scale for Children-V (WISC-V) and the Wechsler Adult Intelligence Scale-IV (WAIS-IV), are the most widely used tests and are used here as an example. They have a great deal of empirical support.

The Wechsler scales assume a normal distribution of intelligence in the population, that is, that intelligence is distributed in the population on a bell curve with most people being in the average range, at the top of the curve, and fewer people well above or well below average, at the edges of the curve. The Wechsler scales include several different subtests, each measuring specific cognitive abilities, and results are combined into index scores and an overall score, or Full Scale IQ (Intelligence Quotient, a ratio between intellect and age). The mean score is 100, and the standard deviation is 15. Approximately 2.5% of the population scores two standard deviations above the mean, and the same percentage scores two standard deviations below the mean. The 2.5% of individuals who score approximately 70 or below are the group of people considered intellectually disabled, presuming they meet the other criteria for the diagnosis, deficits in adaptive functioning and onset in childhood or adolescence.

MEASUREMENT ERROR

For all tests of intellectual functioning, scores are estimates of a true score, rather than the exact true score, because of the presence of measurement error when testing human subjects. The true score lies within a range of scores. One can say with confidence, for example, that there is a 95% chance that a test subject's true score is between 94 and 106 if he or she obtains a Full Scale IQ of 100. On any given day, there is a 95% chance that he or she would score between a 94 and a 106, assuming all else is held constant.

Thus, an IQ score of 71, like that obtained by Freddie Lee Hall, is correctly interpreted as a true score which lies between 68 and 76, based on a 95% confidence interval (Wechsler, 2008). The lower end of the confidence interval falls in the range of mild intellectual disability. The upper end does not. However, an individual with an IQ of 71 meets DSM-5 diagnostic criteria for mild intellectual disability if he or she also has adaptive functioning deficits (see below) and the age of onset of low intellectual functioning was during childhood or adolescence.

The Supreme Court ruled against Florida in Freddie Lee Hall's case because Florida's criteria, which required a fixed score of 70 or below, did not account for measurement error and was inconsistent with standard practice.

FLYNN EFFECT

Another problem that arises when interpreting IQ scores that are close to 70 on an IQ test is the Flynn effect (see Miller, Lovler, & McIntire, 2013). Tests like the Wechsler scales are revised about every 20 years. They are normed correctly, with 100 as the mean and a standard deviation of 15, but over time test scores go up, and someone who would have obtained a score of 100 when the test was first administered will, in general, obtain a higher score in later years of the test.

Thus, if Jane obtains a score of 72 in year 20 of the revision, it would be equivalent to a score of 66 if the test was administered in earlier years (Trahan, Stuebing, Fletcher, & Hiscock, 2014), clearly in the range of mild intellectual disability. In practice, clinicians do not typically correct for the Flynn effect, but there is a great deal of controversy over whether they should in high-stakes situations, such as death penalty cases (Hagan, Drogin, & Guilmette, 2010).

PRACTICE EFFECTS

A third problem that comes up in death penalty and other high-stakes testing situations is the effect of practice. If an IQ test is repeated within a year, certain test scores typically increase because of the impact of practice. If a defendant is given an IQ test in January by the defense, and the same test is repeated six months later by a psychologist for the state, the score on the second administration is likely to be higher (Estevis, Basso, & Combs, 2012). In a case in which the IQ hovers around 70, the increase could make a difference in whether the defendant is exempt from the death penalty.

MALINGERING

Finally, defendants on death row are typically highly motivated to respond to IQ tests in such a way that they are diagnosed with an intellectual disability, so they can avoid execution. They can malinger, that is, make a poor effort and get a low score. However, the diagnosis of intellectual disability is only made if there are deficits in adaptive functioning and if the age of onset was prior to adulthood (in addition to evidence of low intellectual functioning). School and other records might rule out the diagnosis of intellectual disability even when a defendant obtains a low score on an IQ test.

DIAGNOSING INTELLECTUAL DISABILITY: ASSESSMENT OF ADAPTIVE FUNCTIONING

In addition to a low IQ, the diagnosis of intellectual disability requires deficits in adaptive functioning, such as below average skills in communication, self-care, daily living skills, and social skills. Deficits in adaptive functioning can be determined on the basis of scores on standardized, norm-referenced measures of adaptive functioning. These are tests given to *informants* to complete about someone they know well: a parent could be an informant for a child or a caregiver could be an informant for an adult. Tests of adaptive functioning are administered by interview or in a paper and pencil format. The Vineland Adaptive Behavior Scales-II (VABS-II; Sparrow, Cicchetti, & Balla, 2005) is a good example of a measure of adaptive functioning, but there are others as well. The VABS-II assesses the following domains: communication, daily living skills, and socialization with supplemental scales for motor skills and maladaptive behavior. Each of the domains is subdivided into narrower areas of functioning. To meet diagnostic criteria for mild intellectual disability, the individual must receive a score in the deficit range in at least one area.

For defendants in death penalty cases there are unique problems associated with standardized measures of adaptive functioning. The skills for living in a prison environment are very different than those required for living in the community, so it may not be possible to assess adaptive functioning. In addition, informants may not be available to contribute to the assessment, and if they are available they may be highly motivated to portray the defendant as having a low level of adaptive functioning so he or she will be spared the death penalty.

IS RANDI INTELLECTUALLY DISABLED? A BRIEF CASE STUDY

In this imagined case, the court agreed with the state's position that Randi was not intellectually disabled because the evidence of intellectual disability in childhood was inconsistent, and her IQ score was in a range that could be interpreted as above the cutoff for intellectual disability. In addition, it was not clear that Randi had deficits in adaptive functioning. Randi's attorney was planning to appeal. She was obtaining more evidence of intellectual disability in childhood from Randi's family as well as more evidence that Randi had, and still has, adaptive-functioning challenges consistent with intellectual disability. She also was going to have Randi reevaluated with a different assessment instrument because she believes that practice effects resulted in an increase in Randi's IQ score. She thinks she can make a good case.

CONCLUSION

The assessment of intellectual disability for defendants on death row has extraordinary ramifications. Those inmates who fall in the *gray zone*, where the diagnosis is uncertain, present real problems for assessment, as described above. Psychological testing, especially for IQ, serves a uniquely important role in death penalty cases. There can be a lot of conflict over whether an individual has an intellectual disability, with the state arguing that he or she does not and the defense arguing otherwise. Very small differences in test scores can make a big difference in the outcome of the case, to a far greater extent than in other circumstances.

Even in less dramatic situations, the assessment of disability can be challenging. A few points on an IQ test or on another psychological test can determine if an individual is eligible for certain benefits or services. It is important to remember that the individual is not more or less disabled; instead, he or she meets or doesn't meet a legal standard for disability. The cutoff is socially determined, and to some extent, it is arbitrary.

Discussion Questions

1. If you were asked to evaluate a defendant on death row would you do it? What factors would you consider in making your decision?

2. What are some of the challenges in measuring intellectual functioning in the general population? What additional challenges are there when the stakes are as high as they are for those facing the possibility of execution?

3. Can intelligence be measured fairly and accurately for everyone?

Research Ideas

1. How have concepts of intellectual disability changed over time? Conduct a literature review and discuss the evolution of the concept of intellectual disability from the earliest writing about it until the present.

2. Examine at least two different theoretical views of intellectual functioning and discuss the implications for measurement.

3. What are the challenges in measuring adaptive functioning and how have they been addressed?

References

American Association for Intellectual and Developmental Disabilities (AAIDD). (2017). *Definition of Intellectual Disability*. Retrieved from http://aaidd.org/intellectual-disability/definition#.WfzmJWiPLIV

American Psychiatric Association. (2013). *Diagnostic and statistical manual of mental disorders* (5th ed.). Washington, DC: Author.

Estevis, E., Basso, M. R., & Combs, D. (2012, February). Effects of practice on the Wechsler Adult Intelligence Scale-IV across 3- and 6-month intervals. *Clinical Neuropsychologist, 26*(2), 239–254.

Hagan, L. D., Drogin, E. Y., & Guilmette, T. J. (2010). Science rather than advocacy when reporting IQ scores. *Professional Psychology: Research and Practice, 41*(5), 420–423. doi:10.1037/a0021077

Hall v. Florida, 109 So. 3d 704 (2012). Retrieved from http://www.scotusblog.com/case-files/cases/freddie-lee-hall-v-florida/

Haney, C., Weill, J., & Lynch, M. (2015). The death penalty. In B. Cutler, & P. A. Zapf (Eds.), *APA handbook of forensic psychology, Vol. 2: Criminal investigation, adjudication, and sentencing outcomes* (pp. 451–510). Washington, DC: American Psychological Association. Retrieved from http://dx.doi.org/10.1037/14462-017

Miller, L. A., Lovler, R. L., & McIntire, S. A. (2013). *Foundations of psychological testing: A practical approach* (4th ed.). Thousand Oaks, CA: Sage.

Social Security Administration. (n.d.). *Disability Evaluation Under Social Security*. Retrieved from https://www.ssa.gov/disability/professionals/bluebook/12.00-MentalDisorders-Adult.htm#12_05

Sparrow, S. S., Cicchetti, D. V., & Balla, D. A. (2005). *The Vineland Adaptive Behavior Scales-II The Vineland Adaptive Behavior Scales-II.* London, UK: Pearson.

Trahan, L. H., Stuebing, K. K., Fletcher, J. M., & Hiscock, M. (2014, June). The Flynn effect: A meta-analysis. *Psychological Bulletin, 140*(5), 1332–1360.

Wechsler, D. (2008). *WAIS-IV Administration and Scoring Manual*. San Antonio, TX: Pearson.

9

PSYCHOLOGICAL TESTING IN THE WORKPLACE

Selecting Police Officers

LEARNING OBJECTIVES

- Describe the significance of the *Griggs v. Duke Power* case for psychological testing for employee selection

- Describe the impact of the Americans with Disabilities Act on psychological testing for employee selection

- Describe the challenges of conducting validation research for tests used in the selection of police officers

- Explain how test revisions impact validity

- Describe three ethical issues to consider when using psychological tests for selecting police officers

- Define *response bias* and discuss how it impacts psychological testing with prospective police officers and other job applicants

Elinore wanted to be a police officer since she was in middle school. Her father and uncle were police officers, and her mother was a dispatcher, so she knew a lot about the job. She also knew she would have to take psychological tests once she passed the initial phase of the application process. Her father told her not to worry about the tests, but she was a little worried anyway. She didn't know if she should answer questions honestly or if she should try to make herself look like the perfect candidate for the job. She really wanted to be hired.

Dr. Marcos, an organizational psychologist, was responsible for the testing program of the police department. He was knowledgeable about legal hiring practices as well as about police culture and the needs of the department. As part of the testing program he ran, once applicants were offered conditional employment they had to undergo medical and psychological evaluation to ensure they were well suited for a position as a police officer. He had Elinore and the other job candidates complete a personality test, the MMPI-2, along with a police department oriented test of cognitive and academic skills. They took the tests online in a supervised setting, and Dr. Marcos would review the results to make sure all the candidates who were hired were suitable for police work.

THE RELEVANCE OF PSYCHOLOGICAL TESTING TO POLICE WORK

The last few years were particularly troubling ones for police officers in the news, but portrayals of good and bad cops have been plentiful in life and at the movies for years. *Serpico*, the 1973 Oscar winning film, portrays the true story of a New York City police officer, Frank Serpico, who discovered corruption among his colleagues and blew the whistle on them to his own detriment. He was shot by drug dealers in a setup by other police officers, but he survived and testified before the Knapp Commission, a panel convened in New York City in 1970 to investigate police corruption. Stacey Koon and Laurence Powell are the two former Los Angeles Police Department officers who were convicted in the 1991 beating of Rodney King, videotaped by a bystander and shown throughout the world. Their acquittal in state court led to riots in Los Angeles, and they were later convicted in federal court of violating Rodney King's civil rights. In the Danziger Bridge shootings of 2005, police officers in New Orleans, six days after Hurricane Katrina, shot and killed two unarmed men and wounded four other people. They attempted to cover up the shootings by presenting false information. Five police officers were convicted in federal court of crimes related to the shootings in 2011.

These are three of the most notorious and extreme examples of police misconduct in the United States in recent history. However, police corruption, police brutality, and racially biased policing are everyday problems. In February of 2013, for example, *CBS News* reported that 10 metropolitan Atlanta police officers were charged with taking bribes from drug dealers in exchange for allowing them to continue to distribute cocaine. In March 2013, the Miami Herald reported that two police officers were fired following an incident of police brutality that took place three years earlier. They were arrested for badly beating two men, leaving one unconscious and the other disfigured. Racially biased policing has been suspected as a cause of police brutality in some widely publicized cases, but it also underlies racial profiling, in which people of color are targeted for investigation and enforcement in a discriminatory manner. In October 2012, a settlement was reached with the city of East Haven, Connecticut, after an investigation was conducted alleging a pattern of discrimination against Latinos by East Haven police officers. Four officers were arrested and charged, and the chief of police stepped down as part of the settlement.

The Knapp Commission, from the Serpico case, recommended improving selection procedures for police officers, among other recommended changes to the New York City police department. Can psychological testing, as part of the hiring process, contribute to the prevention of police misconduct? Can psychological tests screen out police officers who are likely to become corrupt or engage in police brutality?

Psychological testing is a routine activity in the workplace. Each day across the United States and in other countries, psychological tests are used to hire and promote employees, to develop and coach executives, and to make sure employees are *fit for duty* after an illness or crisis. This chapter considers the use of psychological tests in hiring police officers, as one example of how psychological tests are used in the workplace. Psychologists have been helping to select police officers since at least the 1930s, when the General Adaptability Test was developed for that purpose (Barnette et al., 1950). By 1954, at least one psychologist was using psychological tests to screen applicants to a large police department (Reese, 1995), and by 1967, a couple of years before the Knapp Commission was convened, the President's Commission on Law Enforcement and the Administration of Justice recommended that police departments use psychological tests to evaluate applicants.

Psychological testing for the purpose of selecting police officers is *high-stakes* testing because test results, along with other information, determine whether an applicant is hired. It is also in the public eye because performance problems of police officers are often newsworthy events. In addition, psychological testing for the purpose of employee selection can be the target of lawsuits brought by individuals who were not selected for a coveted position and by organizations representing groups of individuals who believe they were discriminated against in the hiring process. Conversely, failing to use psychological tests for selection of employees can result in charges of negligence in hiring (see *Bonsignore v. City of New York*, 1981; *Woods v. Town of Danville, WV*, 2010). These issues are of concern to the public as it is in the public interest to have an effective police force and because taxpayers are ultimately responsible for legal costs associated with problems created by local, state, or federal employees.

PSYCHOLOGICAL TESTS AND THE SELECTION OF POLICE OFFICERS: AN INTRODUCTION

There are about 800,000 police officers in the United States (Bureau of Labor Statistics, 2017). Police officers have the authority to deprive citizens of their individual rights and to use deadly force to accomplish their goals. They have access to confidential information and confiscated items. They work with the public including people who are irate, distressed, or mentally ill. Sometimes they have to make decisions in moments, with very serious consequences, without consulting anyone or getting permission from a superior, but they also have to follow the law and a strict chain of command.

Along with appropriate training, good working conditions, and structures that minimize the likelihood of police misconduct, smart hiring practices contribute to a safe and effective police force. Many large police departments have psychologists on staff who evaluate police recruits as a primary job responsibility, using tests, interviews, and reviews of background information, while other departments hire external consultants to perform the same function.

Unfortunately, psychological testing is not a simple or straightforward solution to the hiring challenges of police departments. It would be easy to administer psychological tests to applicants online, have a computer score them, and make good hiring decisions on the basis of test scores, but it doesn't work that way. From a legal standpoint, employers must be diligent about not discriminating against groups of people protected by civil rights laws. Discrimination on the basis of age, race, color, sex, national origin, religion, disability, or genetic information is illegal in the United States and many other countries. Unless a psychological test can be shown to fulfill a genuine business need, it cannot be used in employee selection if its use results in discrimination. Furthermore, to be used in an employment context, psychological tests must predict job performance.

This chapter considers both of these issues, the legal and the scientific, as well as ethical guidelines, as they relate to the use of psychological tests in selecting police officers.

LEGAL CONSIDERATIONS

An applicant for a job at Duke Energy (then called Duke Power) in 1970, for any position other than the lowest paid, would have been required to take a cognitive ability test, a test that is intended to evaluate intelligence. Until the 1960s, African Americans were only permitted to work for the lowest paying department at Duke, by design. After the Civil Rights Act of 1964 was passed by Congress, outlawing employment discrimination on the basis of race, Duke changed their policies so that better paid employees at Duke were required to possess a high school diploma and to have at least average scores on a standardized cognitive ability test. African Americans were much less likely to have graduated from high school and also less likely to score at the acceptable level on the cognitive ability test, allowing Duke Power to continue to employ Blacks in the lowest paying positions, while promoting White employees to higher paying positions.

Thirteen African American employees, represented by lawyers from the NAACP Legal Defense Fund (LDF), took Duke Power to court and prevailed in a landmark case that was decided in 1971, *Griggs v. Duke Power*. Duke Power could not show that its employment testing practices fulfilled a genuine business need. Whites who had not graduated from high school and scored below average on cognitive ability tests but held the positions in question prior to the change in Duke's policies performed as well as those who met the new criteria. Duke Power was required to change its employment testing practices to make them a valid measure of applicants' abilities to perform the job in question. The *Griggs v. Duke Power* case transformed the way employers use psychological tests for employee selection.

Adverse impact, a legal and technical term that arose out of civil rights legislation, is defined as a substantial difference in the rate of selection in hiring (or other employment decisions) that disadvantages members of groups protected by civil rights laws. Adverse impact occurs when hiring practices, including psychological testing, result in a selection rate for the protected group that is less than 80% of the selection rate for the group with the highest selection rate. For example, if a test results in the selection of 45 out of 100 Black applicants and 90 out of 100 White applicants (assuming that Whites in this instance have the highest selection rate), it would be considered discriminatory against Blacks, a protected group under civil rights law, because the selection rate for Blacks is half the selection rate for Whites (50%, well below the 80% rule). In order to engage in a hiring practice that has an adverse impact, a company has to show that there is a business need for the practice and that there is no method of satisfying the business need that has less of an adverse impact.

A related legal concern about personality testing for employee selection is the impact of personality testing on individuals who have mental health problems and are therefore protected from discrimination by the Americans with Disabilities Act (ADA). Inquiring about mental health problems or emotional stability in preemployment screening is explicitly prohibited by the ADA (Camara & Merenda, 2000). The MMPI-2 and other clinically focused personality tests are intended to reveal psychopathology and their use is prohibited in preemployment screening. When these kinds of tests fulfill a genuine business need, however, such as excluding candidates who are emotionally unstable from a public safety position, they can be administered after a conditional job offer is made to the applicant. A conditional job offer is one that requires the applicant to meet further conditions, for example, obtaining a positive recommendation from the psychologist, in order to be hired.

Another legal issue related to conducting psychological testing in the workplace, unrelated to discrimination, is the job applicant's right to privacy. Psychological testing in the workplace came under examination in Senate and Congressional subcommittee hearings due to concerns about employees' right to privacy in 1965 (Buchanan, 2002). At that time, the MMPI, which asked test takers to respond to hundreds of very specific questions, was used by the federal government for employee selection and a lot of people, both liberals and conservatives, were concerned about it. Some people found questions on the MMPI offensive, and others worried that responses to specific questions would be maintained in personnel files. In this particular case, Congressional hearings concluded that there was no evidence of widespread invasion of privacy or misuse of the MMPI by federal agencies (Amrine, 1965; Buchanan, 2002) because the MMPI was used in instances where emotional stability of employees was paramount, for example, for entrance into the Peace Corps and for some positions in the Department of Defense.

In 1989, Target was sued for violating privacy laws in California when the company conducted preemployment testing for security guards (*Soroka v. Dayton Hudson Corporation*). As part of the selection process, job applicants were asked to take a test based in part on the MMPI. The test included questions the plaintiffs felt violated their privacy, such as questions about religious belief and sexual orientation, and they argued that the right to be free from "unreasonable intrusions into areas and interests deemed to be private" was guaranteed by the California Constitution (Camara & Merenda, 2000). The Appellate Court concluded that there must be a compelling reason for any violation of the right to privacy. In other words, there must be a good reason, a genuine business need, to violate the privacy of job applicants by asking intrusive questions.

Complicating matters, the right to privacy, when based on the Fourth Amendment of the United States Constitution, which prohibits unreasonable search and seizure by the federal government, applies to federal employers, not to state, municipal, or private employers. However, some states have right to privacy laws in their state constitutions, and these apply to state employees and may also apply to private employers, as they do in California.

The Uniform Guidelines on Employee Selection Procedures was adopted in 1978 by several federal agencies and commissions, including the Equal Employment Opportunity Commission and the Department of Labor. The Uniform Guidelines cover a range of hiring practices including both cognitive and personality testing and outline specific requirements and practices for employee selection. For example, the Uniform Guidelines discuss the relationship between discrimination and selection procedures, record keeping requirements, and acceptable types of validity studies. Psychologists who administer tests for selecting police officers need to be mindful of the guidelines as they decide on evaluation strategies.

ETHICAL CONSIDERATIONS

Psychological tests can cause harm. In the employee selection context, they can be used to exclude people from jobs unfairly and unnecessarily. They can also be fraudulent; unvalidated tests can be promoted as predictive of future behaviors that they don't predict. The American Psychological Association's (APA) Code of Ethics offers guidelines for the practice of psychological testing and assessment, and the APA also publishes the Standards for Educational and Psychological Testing, which issues standards for test development and use. It was last published in 2014.

A basic APA ethical standard is that psychologists only provide services within the boundaries of their competence (APA, 2002). Competence is a significant issue in police psychology, which became a recognized area of specialization, or proficiency, within the APA in 2013. It is vital for psychologists who conduct assessments of police officer candidates to have specialized training and practical experience in police psychology (Gallo & Halgin, 2011). They need to have specific knowledge about police officers' working conditions, stressors, and functions in addition to having expertise in assessment. They also must be culturally competent. That is, they need to have cultural self-awareness, culturally appropriate clinical skills, and knowledge about diverse cultures, specifically, police culture, cultures of the populations served by the police department they are hiring for, and the cultures of individual applicants (Goldfinger & Pomerantz, 2014; Johnson, 2011). A psychologist who is culturally competent also recognizes that cultural groups are heterogeneous and not every individual who is a member of the group is alike (Goldfinger & Pomerantz, 2014).

Another ethical standard dictates that psychologists take precautions to protect confidential information, including test and interview data and evaluation reports (APA, 2002). Psychologists who conduct evaluations to select police officers are likely to gather more information than is essential to make hiring decisions, and they need to minimize intrusions on an applicant's privacy as they consider the questions they ask in the interview and the information that should go into the report. They also need to think about who within the agency should have access to the information, how to ensure that the confidentiality of the job applicant is protected throughout the evaluation process, and how to ensure the confidentiality of the job applicant when the test data is stored. In an informed consent procedure, at the start of the process, they must let the applicant know that he or she will not have access to test results, the usual approach in employment-related testing situations but contrary to ethical requirements in most other circumstances.

Finally, psychologists need to use tests "whose validity and reliability have been established for use with members of the population tested" and base their opinions on "information and techniques sufficient to substantiate their findings" (APA, 2002, p. 1071). These are basic requirements for assessment and are well covered by recommended practices for evaluating police applicants, such as relying on more than one test as well as an interview and review of background information before making decisions about an applicant, as will be seen below.

CURRENT PRACTICES

According to Dantzker (2011), "There is no nationally recognized and generally followed set of recommendations as to what questionnaire(s) or evaluative protocols should be used in doing preemployment screening of law enforcement officers" (p. 276). He concludes, after reviewing the literature, that an assessment battery (a group of psychological tests) for the selection of police officers should include both personality and cognitive ability testing. However, he indicates that the specific tests that should be used remain open to debate. Gallo and Halgin (2011), in the same volume of the journal, suggest a test battery that includes the MMPI-2 and the Rotter Incomplete Sentences Blank (a brief projective test) to identify psychopathology, the California Psychological Inventory (CPI) to gather information about normal personality traits, the Inwald Personality Inventory (IPI) to assess characteristics important to police work, and the Wonderlic Cognitive Ability Test. Other psychologists choose among several tests that have gone through extensive validation studies specific to selecting police officers. These will be discussed in more detail below.

International Association of Chiefs of Police (IACP) guidelines (Ben-Porath et al., 2011) recommend that psychologists use at least two objectively scored psychological tests that are validated for screening for public safety positions. The tests should be relevant to assessing emotional stability as well as factors that are predictive of good performance. They further recommend that tests are followed by an in-person, semistructured interview to clarify and further interpret test results and by a review of information gathered from a background investigation, polygraph report, or discussion with agency staff. The semistructured interview should cover a range of relevant information, from educational and employment history to family and interpersonal interactions, and it should also include a medical history specific to psychological functioning. Therefore, the interview needs to take place after a conditional offer of employment is made, to comply with the ADA.

Psychologists conduct preemployment evaluations as a relatively small part of comprehensive selection procedures for police officers. Every police department has its own approach. An applicant to the New York City police department, for example, must be between the ages of 17½ and 35 to take an initial entrance exam. The exam tests cognitive ability, observational skills, and mental acuity. Before they are hired, applicants must have 60 college credits or two years of military service and a high school diploma. They also have to live in New York City or the surrounding counties, and they have to pass a background check. Then they go on to physical and medical testing and the psychological evaluation. If they *fail to meet standards* for the physical abilities test, the medical evaluation, or the psychological exam, they are disqualified from entry into the police force. A disqualified applicant can appeal the decision or reapply after a waiting period.

CHOOSING PSYCHOLOGICAL TESTS FOR SELECTING POLICE OFFICERS

Cognitive and Academic Skill Testing

Cognitive ability is essentially intelligence, the ability to think. It comes in many forms, for example, the ability to work quickly, to recall and reorganize information, to understand spatial relationships, to communicate using language, and to think abstractly. Cognitive ability testing, or intelligence testing, is problematic for selecting police officers because it can result in adverse impact to a protected group, as it did in the *Grigg v. Duke* case described above. Scores on general tests of cognitive ability may not have enough of a relationship to performance as a police officer to make up for the possibility of employment discrimination. Academic skill testing is more straightforward. Basic arithmetic, reading, and writing skills are clearly relevant to succeeding at a training program for police officers and for police work.

The National Police Officer Selection Test is one example of an entry exam that tests for the basic skills needed for police work. The National Criminal Justice Officer Selection Inventory (NCJOSI) tests for problem-solving ability and attitude. Both of these tests, and there are others, are specific to the needs of a police force. They are well validated for that purpose (predictive of job performance), and they minimize adverse impact.

Personality Testing

Personality testing is used in police officer selection to choose officers who are likely to be good at their job and also to select out those who are at risk of misconduct. Some personality tests, such as the MMPI-2 and PAI, are used to exclude candidates who are emotionally unstable and to recommend candidates who will be good police officers. Others, such as the NEO Personality Inventory-3 (NEO-3) and CPI, measure normal personality traits, and for hiring purposes, they are focused on selecting for characteristics that make good police officers and selecting out applicants with characteristics that are associated with counterproductive behavior (i.e., lying, antisocial behavior, or lack of follow through).

All of these tests, as well as tests specifically developed for selecting police officers, such as the IPI and the Matrix-Predictive Uniform Law Enforcement Selection Evaluation (M-PULSE), have been specifically validated for use in selecting public safety personnel. That means that the test has been shown to predict job performance for police officers. Most are administered after a conditional offer of employment has been made because of the likelihood that they can detect psychopathology; therefore, they are considered to be a medical exam.

How Is Personality Testing Relevant to the Selection of Police Officers?

We bring our characteristic ways of thinking, feeling, and behaving everywhere we go, including to the workplace. From the lens of the Five-Factor Model of personality (McCrae & Costa, 1997), a well-researched, empirical approach to describing personality traits, if we tend to be disagreeable, disorganized, and anxious outside of work, we will likely be disagreeable, disorganized, and anxious at work.

Are there personality traits that predispose police officers to engage in misconduct, or conversely, are there traits that predispose police officers to be especially good at police work? Can candidates with the propensity toward misconduct, but without a documented history of psychopathology or problem behavior, be identified via psychological tests? What would the test profiles of such individuals look like?

There are a number of challenges in conducting the research to answer these questions. First, documented police officer misconduct occurs infrequently; it is a low base rate phenomenon. Most applicants who are likely to engage in misconduct are screened out early in the selection process and never become police officers, and others who engage in misconduct while on the police force are never caught. Psychological tests have to cast a wide net to predict few instances of misconduct. In addition, police officers who engage in misconduct could have very different profiles of test results. For example, some incidents of police brutality or corruption might arise out of problem personality characteristics, such as antisocial traits or pathological narcissism, while others could stem from temporary lapses in judgment and self-control fueled by drug problems. Other incidents of misconduct could be related to low assertiveness, bending to a corrupt police subculture.

Also, police departments vary in their needs and how they function. They have different training programs, cultures, management styles, and quality and levels of supervision. A good police officer in one setting might be ineffective in another. Conversely, an officer prone to misconduct might be able to exercise self-control in some police departments, while in others, the same officer could exhibit significant problem behaviors. In some agencies, misconduct among police officers could be allowed to fester; for example, use of excessive force might be overlooked or new police officers might be trained in minor acts of corrupt policing by veteran officers, as apparently happened in New York City prior to the Knapp Commission investigation. In other departments, training programs and supervisory structures help new police officers with a wide range of personality characteristics become adept at police work. Finally, people change over time and with experience. In fact, one of the recommendations coming out of the Christopher Commission that followed the Rodney King incident is to regularly reevaluate police officers. Experience on the police force and elsewhere, aging, and health problems, especially those affecting brain functioning, can change personality characteristics relevant to police work.

What has research shown so far? Anxiety contributes to vehicular reprimands (when an officer is disciplined for violating vehicle-related safety policies), and impulsivity contributes to reprimands for use of excessive force, as measured by the MMPI-2 and other instruments (Beutler, Storm, Kirkish, Scogin, & Gaines, 1985). An "immaturity index" of the MMPI predicts termination from small town police departments (Bartol, 1991, p. 130); lack of assertiveness as measured by the IPI predicts poorly rated officers or those who were terminated from police departments in Appalachia (Mufson, 1998); high scores on the L scale of the MMPI-2 predicts performance problems of police officers (Weiss, Vivian, Weiss, Davis, & Rostow, 2013). Weiss and Weiss (2011), in their review of research related to the validity of the MMPI-2, PAI, CPI, IPI, and M-PULSE for selection of police officers, indicate that individuals scoring high in tolerance and intellectual efficiency on the CPI tend to perform well in police work (Aamodt, 2004), while those with high scores on the Antisocial, Borderline features, and drug use scales of the PAI are likely to have performance problems (Weiss, Hitchcock, Weiss, Rostow, & Davis, 2008). These are some examples of research on personality factors related to performance of police officers, a still very active area of research using a variety of personality tests. Taken together, they suggest that immaturity, antisocial attitudes, grandiosity, a history of drug abuse, problematic interpersonal relationships, and naïve denial of common shortcomings can be evaluated by psychological tests in some instances and are associated with problems in police work. In contrast, individuals who are nonjudgmental and clear thinking, all else being equal, are likely to perform well as police officers.

How Are Personality Characteristics Measured?

How do we measure impulsivity, antisocial attitudes, and all of the other personality characteristics that might influence the behavior of police officers? Can we measure these characteristics reliably in a high-stakes testing situation such as employee selection?

For the purpose of employee selection, personality is most often measured through norm-referenced, standardized, empirically supported self-report tests such as the MMPI-2. For these kinds of tests, job applicants answer a series of questions about themselves in a written format with limited options for responding; for example, they may be given response options including True/False, or never, sometimes, often, and always. For the MMPI-2, job applicants answer over 500 questions by responding true or false. Their responses are tabulated, resulting in scores on a number of scales, and their scaled scores are compared to those of a normative group, either a representative sample of adults in the United States or more specific norm groups, as discussed below. The resulting profile is interpreted by a professional who is knowledgeable about test interpretation, personality, and the needs of the police force.

The MMPI-2 and its precursor, the MMPI, have been measuring personality in this way since the 1940s. Current application of the MMPI-2 often considers scores on individual scales and two or three point *code types* as a reflection of personality characteristics (Groth-Marnat, 2009), although the test also continues to be used to detect emotional instability and psychopathology. The NEO-3, to take another example, compares an individual's scores on 30 scales with scores taken from a normal population rather than scores of people who have mental health problems or other forms of psychopathology. The NEO-3 measures normal personality traits, those we are all thought to share to a greater or lesser extent.

Both the MMPI-2 and the NEO-3 have a great deal of research support behind them, indicating that they reliably measure the characteristics that they intend to measure. There are several other personality tests that also have strong empirical support, such as the PAI, CPI, and Sixteen Personality Factor Questionnaire (16 PF). All of these have been used successfully in selecting police officers. The M-PULSE Inventory (Davis & Rostow, 2008) and the IPI are a little different than the others although they are also well-researched self-report measures of personality characteristics. They were designed specifically to use in selecting public safety personnel such as police officers.

Self-report personality tests are both efficient and effective, but they are limited. Test takers have to choose from options that are provided for them. This makes the test straightforward to score and makes scoring objective. However, it doesn't allow for the richness and depth that can come from an open-ended inquiry. Also, test takers can only respond to test items based on what they know about themselves, and they choose what to report and what to deny. Test results are vulnerable to attempts at impression management and might not accurately reflect personality characteristics of the test taker. Another concern is that security issues could arise with self-report tests. Applicants can be coached to respond to test items in a particular manner to get the outcome they desire.

Projective or performance based personality tests, such as the Rorschach Inkblot Method and Thematic Apperception Test (TAT), allow test takers to respond to structured stimuli without limiting their options. Projective tests are more difficult and time consuming to administer and score than self-report tests, and they are very controversial among psychologists, many of whom believe they lack sufficient validity to be used in applied settings. However, they may be less susceptible to impression management than self-report tests (Weiss & Weiss, 2008). Projective tests were commonly used for employee selection in the past and are probably still being used for employee selection by some psychologists. New developments in performance-based personality tests, such as the Rorschach Performance Assessment System (RPAS), could make projective or performance-based tests more valuable for selecting public safety employees in the future.

Validating Personality Tests for Use in Police Officer Selection

To establish evidence of the validity of a personality test for selecting police officers, researchers must demonstrate that the test can predict future behavior. That is ultimately the purpose of administering the test. The researcher must determine the behaviors that need to be measured, the markers for good or poor performance of police officers. These are the criterion variables for the validity study. Research studies have used a variety of criterion variables, including supervisor ratings on characteristics rated as important to the department, early termination from the police force, and reprimands or other disciplinary actions. Each approach has strengths and weaknesses. For example, supervisor ratings may be very relevant to performance, but they also could be biased, and disciplinary actions are objective evidence of behavior, but not all police misconduct results in disciplinary action.

The researcher has to formulate hypotheses about predictor and criterion variables and determine how to measure the predictor variables, the personality characteristics or other factors that are hypothesized to predict the criterion variable. For example, high scores on the Neuroticism scale of the NEO-3 could be hypothesized to predict early termination from the police force, for theoretical reasons or due to results of previous research. Then the researcher collects the data needed to determine whether the hypothesis is borne out by the data.

Those who conduct research on the selection of police officers typically conduct applied research; they don't perform experiments. That is, they make use of naturally collected data or collect additional data in the course of routine selection work. They do not, and cannot, conduct experiments that randomly assign members of the general population, job seekers, or even police recruits, to experimental and control groups to collect data for research purposes.

An important complication in validity studies is that revised versions of a test cannot be assumed to predict job performance as well as the previous version of the test. When the MMPI was revised and became the MMPI-2, in 1989, findings from all of the validation studies for the original MMPI did not transfer to the MMPI-2. It was a different test. A revised form of the MMPI-2, the MMPI-2-RF, was published in 2008. It is shorter than the MMPI-2, and some of the scales have been reconstructed. It will take time to complete the additional validation studies that are needed for the MMPI-2-RF to be as accepted as the MMPI-2, especially for high-stakes testing such as employee selection.

There are other complications as well. Since the ADA rules took effect, most tests can only be administered after applicants have been offered conditional employment. Also, it is not acceptable to hire someone who does poorly on a test for a public safety position and then see how he or she does on the job. These issues have led to technical challenges in validating psychological tests for the purpose of police officer selection. By the time the tests are administered, most applicants who would be screened out have already been screened out based on background information or other collected data, and those who do poorly on a test are not offered a job. That leaves a very restricted range of test scores to conduct studies on. Very few of the test protocols (which contain the predictor variables) will include elevated scores on any scales, and very few individuals who are ultimately hired will have poor supervisor ratings or disciplinary problems (criterion variables). Thus, both predictor and criterion variables have a limited range. If everybody gets close to the same score, the scores are not going to be able to predict much of anything (see Miller, Lovler, & McIntire, 2013), so that validity studies related to job performance are likely to come up with validation coefficients that are low. However, validation coefficients can be statistically adjusted for the restricted range of test scores (Miller et al., 2013) and even small effect sizes can be meaningful in the context of employee selection for public safety positions (Weiss & Weiss, 2011).

Normative Groups

One important consideration in selecting police officers is to recognize that people who seek careers in the police force are a self-selected group. Interpreting test results using normative data for the general population could be misleading because of the unique qualities of police recruits. As noted by Miller et al. (2013), "The person who interprets test scores must choose the norm group that most closely resembles the test takers" (p. 146). Interpreting test results using normative data for the general population is also misleading because job candidates for all kinds of positions are motivated to respond defensively to test items.

For these reasons, most psychological tests used in selecting police officers have norms specific to law enforcement candidates. For example, software for the PAI, a self-report measure of personality characteristics and psychopathology, offers a law enforcement interpretive module that compares profiles of police officer candidates with those of other public safety applicants as well as those of applicants who went on to successful employment in public safety positions for more than a year. The PAI has normative groups that are very specific, including dispatchers, firefighters, and corrections officers. Similarly, an interpretive report for law enforcement for the MMPI-2 compares candidates' profiles with job applicants in general, job applicants for law enforcement positions, and law enforcement personnel. The NEO-PI-R, or NEO Personality Inventory-Revised, has newly published norms for police officer applicants (Detrick & Chibnall, 2013), although these are based on a small sample (and the NEO-PI-R was recently revised). Note that the PAI, the MMPI-2, and the NEO are designed for use with general populations and have much broader applicability than law enforcement selection.

The M-PULSE Inventory (Davis & Rostow, 2004) measures attitudes, values, beliefs, and behaviors relevant to law enforcement job performance for the purpose of predicting officer misconduct. Results of the M-PULSE Inventory are combined with results of an interview, background questionnaire, brief cognitive ability testing, and the MMPI-2 using an actuarial method (a method based on statistical probabilities); a report is generated that specifies whether an applicant is a liability risk and why. The probabilities for risk of misconduct are based on comparing the profiles of job candidates with the profiles of police officers who engaged in misconduct.

Similarly, the IPI and recently, the IPI-2, were designed to screen candidates for public safety positions and focus on assessing antisocial behavior and psychopathology. Results are interpreted using normative data from public safety and security personnel and intended to be used in conjunction with an interview. The IPI is sometimes used in conjunction with the MMPI-2.

Response Bias in Personality Testing for the Selection of Police Officers

In high-stakes testing, such as testing for hiring purposes, applicants are motivated to look their best. It is difficult to measure problematic personality characteristics that people know about but want to hide. Similarly, job applicants may purposefully respond to questions in a way that makes them seem better than they are, for example, more reliable and motivated than is in fact the case. Job candidates may underreport symptoms and problems, such as mistrusting others, experiencing negative emotions, and having interpersonal challenges. In addition, they may not be aware of problems or negative personality characteristics and therefore can't acknowledge them. To counteract these problems, the MMPI-2, the PAI, and several other self-report measures of personality employ validity scales intended to assess socially desirable, defensive responding. Some authors recommend having applicants who produce an invalid profile retake the test after being told that they responded defensively, and they often produce a valid profile on readministration (Butcher, 2006).

McGrath, Mitchell, Kim, & Hough (2010) reviewed the literature and failed to find support for the use of validity scales that measure positive impression management or socially desirable responding. They examined research studies that asked whether elevated scores on impression management scales had an impact on elevations on other scales, the substantive scales. They found little evidence of impression management (response bias) in studies of people who had low motivation to distort their responses. They also found little evidence that response bias had an effect on scores on substantive scales in work-related settings, where people had a lot of motivation to distort their responses. They conclude that "what is troubling about the failure to find consistent support for bias indicators is the extent to which they are regularly used in high-stakes circumstances, such as employee selection or hearings to evaluate competence to stand trial and sanity" (McGrath et al., 2010, p. 465).

Other authors dispute their conclusions (see Rohling et al., 2011). However, even these authors concede that McGrath and his colleagues' (2010) conclusions might apply to the indicators of socially desirable responding used in industrial-organizational settings, such as for selecting employees.

Despite the findings of McGrath et al. (2010) about validity scales, research supports the use of at least some validity indicators in the selection of police officers. Weiss et al. (2013) analyzed data from over 4,000 police officers and found that officers who obtained L-scale scores on the MMPI-2 of eight or higher had significantly more performance problems as working police officers than those with scores of seven or lower. The L scale, or *Lie* scale, of the MMPI-2 consists of 15 items, and a high score on the L scale indicates that the test taker responded to these items in a manner suggesting he or she naively attempted to make a favorable impression.

Whether it is possible to manipulate one's responses to self-report tests, that is, to fake, distort, cheat, or otherwise *game* the system to present oneself in a more positive light than is warranted without it being discovered, and the consequences of distorted responding, continue to be controversial issues in employee selection. Note, however, that similar problems can arise in interviews and when reviewing resumes, two essential components of the hiring process.

INTERPRETATION AND COMMUNICATION OF TEST RESULTS

Test results used in the selection of police officers are usually interpreted with the assistance of computer-based interpretive software. Computer-based test interpretation (CBTI) reports provide descriptions of typical individuals who have patterns of test scores—they don't describe an individual person. It is up to the psychologist to integrate the information offered in the report with other relevant data, such as background information and information collected in the interview, and it is also up to the psychologist to draw conclusions from the CBTI reports and other data.

After collecting all of the data, psychologists have to incorporate it into a report with their recommendations about hiring. The report must be prepared in a manner that will stand up in court, because an applicant who is denied a position on the basis of the psychological evaluation may sue the psychologist for discrimination or incompetence (Craig, 2005). The evaluation report needs to meet the same standards as other forensic reports, those that are prepared for legal purposes. It needs to include, for example, a statement indicating that the applicant was provided information about the limits to their confidentiality and other factors relevant to informed consent, information about the procedures involved in the evaluation, and information about relevant codes and statutes, especially minimum selection standards or codes that specify competencies required for police officers.

In discussing test results, the report may refer to research-based interpretations of test data and also to "miss rates" of the test (Johnson, 2011), information that is relevant to demonstrating that the tests used in the evaluation can predict job performance. It may also refer to the particular norms used to interpret the test data and why they were chosen.

The report needs to address the specific concerns of the hiring agency. For example, the report could contain a statement about how well the applicant is likely to engage with different groups served by the agency. Regardless of the questions answered in the report, the opinions of the psychologist must be backed up by data and also qualified in terms of the level of certainty, or uncertainty, of the findings. The report has to draw a conclusion, which are the psychologist's opinion in regard to the suitability of the applicant for the position he or she applied for. The reasoning for the opinion should be clear from the information provided in the body of the report.

ELINORE AND ELENA: DIFFERENT TEST RESULTS LEAD TO DIFFERENT OUTCOMES

Although she never got any feedback about her test scores, Elinore was hired as a police officer for the same department her father worked for. She was nervous but also thrilled to start her career. Dr. Marco had the unfortunate job of telling a different candidate, Elena, that she was not going to be hired. He wrote Elena a letter and invited her to contact him if she wanted to discuss the findings. Her test scores indicated that she likely had a mood disorder and a lot of anxiety, and the results suggested that she would have a lot of difficulty in a police officer position. In the letter, Dr. Marcos informed Elena about other jobs within the department that would be open to her, and he also advised her that she had a right to an appeal and that she could reapply for a police officer position in a year. However, he hoped for her sake that Elena would get treatment and choose a less stressful line of work.

CONCLUSION

Psychological testing for personnel selection presents challenging legal, ethical, and scientific issues, as was shown in this review of the use of psychological testing in hiring police officers. Psychological testing for basic cognitive and academic abilities is straightforward, as long as the instruments used do not result in discrimination. Evaluating applicants to select out those with serious psychopathology is also usually straightforward, using tests, interview data, and background information. However, using tests to select out those applicants who are at risk for misconduct and to select in those who would make effective police officers for a given police department is much more complicated. It is an ongoing effort to determine what scores on which tests predict police misconduct. The stakes are high for applicants and also for the public.

Discussion Questions

1. Imagine you are responsible for hiring employees for a large corporation. Would you use psychological tests as part of the selection process? Why or why not?

2. How can the selection process for police officers be improved? What are the pros and cons of using psychological tests in the selection of police officers?

3. Discuss the impediments to conducting research on psychological testing in selecting police officers. What additional research would improve the selection process? How can research on this topic be conducted so that it does not jeopardize public safety?

Research Ideas

1. Review the literature on psychological testing in leadership development or executive coaching. Discuss which tests are useful, how they are used, and if their use is adequately supported by research.

2. Review the research on integrity testing for employee selection. How is it used?

   How are integrity tests developed and validated?

3. Review the research on validity scales in psychological testing. When are validity scales useful?

References

Aamodt, M. G. (2004). *Law enforcement selection: Research summaries*. Washington, DC: Police Executive Research Forum.

Amrine, M. (1965). The 1965 Congressional Inquiry into Testing: A Commentary. *American Psychologist,* *20*(11), 859–870. Retrieved from http://dx.doi.org/10.1037/h0021343

American Psychological Association. (2002). Ethical principles of psychologists and code of conduct. *American Psychologist, 57*, 1060–1073.

Barnette, W. L., Jr., Harrell, T. W., Bills, M. A., Lewis, K., Bellows, R. M., O'Rourke, L. J., . . . & Thompson, L. A. (1950). Fields of personnel psychology selection and training. In D. H. Fryer & E. R. Henry (Eds.), *Handbook of applied psychology* (pp. 195-260). Retrieved from http://dx.doi .org/10.1037/11530-005

Bartol, C. R. (1991). Predictive validation of the MMPI for small-town police officers who fail. *Professional Psychology: Research and Practice,* *22*(2), 127–132. Retrieved from http://dx.doi .org/10.1037/0735-7028.22.2.127

Ben-Porath, Y. S., Fico, J. M., Hibler, N. S., Inwald, R., Kruml, J., & Roberts, M. (2011, August). Assessing the psychological suitability of candidates for law enforcement positions. *Police Chief Magazine, 78,* 64–70. Retrieved from http://www.policechiefmagazine.org/magazine/index.cfm?fuseaction=display_arch&article_id=2448&issue_id=82011

Beutler, L. E., Storm, A., Kirkish, P., Scogin, F., & Gaines, J. A. (1985). Parameters in the prediction of police officer performance. *Professional Psychology: Research and Practice,* *16*(2), 324–335. Retrieved from http://dx.doi .org/10.1037/0735-7028.16.2.324

Bonsignore v. City of New York, 683 F. 2d 635 (1982).

Buchanan, R. D. (2002). On not "giving psychology away": The Minnesota Multiphasic Inventory and public controversy over testing in the 1960s. *History of Psychology, 5*(3), 284–309.

Bureau of Labor Statistics, U.S. Department of Labor. (2017). *Occupational outlook handbook, 2016-17 edition, police and detectives.* Retrieved from https://www.bls.gov/ooh/protectiveservice/police-and-detectives.htm

Butcher, J. N. (Ed.). (2006). *MMPI-2: A practitioner's guide.* Washington, DC: American Psychological Association.

Camara, W. J., & Merenda, P. F. (2000). Using personality tests in preemployment screening: Issues raised in *Soroka v. Dayton Hudson Corporation. Psychology, Public Policy, and Law,* *6*(4), 1164–1186.

Craig, R. (2005). *Personality-guided forensic psychology.* Washington, DC: American Psychological Association.

Dantzker, M. L. (2011). Psychological preemployment screening for police candidates: Seeking consistency if not standardization. *Professional Psychology: Research and Practice, 42*(3), 276–283. doi:10.1037/a0023736

Davis, R. D., & Rostow, C. D. (2004). Using MMPI special scale configurations to predict law enforcement officers fired for cause. *Applied H.R.M. Research, 9*(1–2), 57–58.

Detrick, P., & Chibnall, J. T. (2013, November). Revised NEO personality inventory normative data for police officer selection. *Psychological Services, 10*(4), 372–377. doi:10.1037/a0031800

Gallo, F. J., & Halgin, R. P. (2011). A guide for establishing a practice in police preemployment post offer psychological evaluations. *Professional Psychology: Research and Practice, 42*(3), 269–275. Retrieved from http://dx.doi .org/10.1037/a0022493

Goldfinger, K., & Pomerantz, A. M. (2014). *Psychological assessment and report-writing.* Thousand Oaks, CA: Sage.

Griggs v. Duke Power Co., 401 U.S. 424 (1971)

Groth-Marnat, G. (2009). Handbook of psychological assessment (5th ed.). Hoboken, NJ: John Wiley.

Johnson, R. (2011). The integration section of forensic psychological evaluation reports in law enforcement: Culturally responsive ending words. In J. Kitaeff (Ed.), *The handbook of police psychology.* New York, NY: Routledge-Taylor.

McCrae, R. R. & Costa, P. T. (1997). Personality trait structure as a human universal. *American Psychologist, 52*(5), 509–516.

McGrath, R. E., Mitchell, M., Kim, B. H., & Hough, L. (2010). Evidence for response bias as a source of error variance in applied assessment. *Psychological Bulletin, 136*(3), 450–470. doi:10.1037/a0019216

Miller, L. A., Lovler, R. L., &McIntire, S. A. (2013) Foundations of psychological testing (4th ed.). Thousand Oaks, CA: Sage.

Mufson, D. W., & Mufson, M. A. (1998, February). Predicting police officer performance using the Inwald personality inventory: An illustration from Appalachia. *Professional Psychology: Research and Practice, 29*(1), 59–62. doi:10.1037/0735-7028.29.1.59

Reese, J. T. (1995). A history of police psychological services. In M. I. Kurke & E. M. Scrivner (Eds.), *Series in applied psychology. Police psychology into the 21st century* (pp. 31–44). Hillsdale, NJ: Lawrence Erlbaum Associates.

Rohling, M. L., Larrabee, G. J., Greiffenstein, M. F., Ben-Porath, Y. S., Lees-Haley, P., Green, P., & Greve, K. W. (2011, July). A misleading review of response bias: Comment on McGrath, Mitchell, Kim, and Hough. *Psychological Bulletin, 137*(4), 708–712. doi:10.1037/a0023327

Weiss, P.A., Hitchcock, J. H., Weiss, W. U., Rostow, C., & Davis, R. (2008, September). The

Personality assessment inventory borderline, drug, and alcohol scales as predictors of overall performance in police officers: A series of exploratory analyses. *Policing & Society, 18*(3), 301–310. Retrieved from http://dx.doi.org/10.1080/10439460802091708

Weiss, P. A., Vivian, J. E., Weiss, W. U., Davis, R. D., & Rostow, C. D. (2013). The MMPI-2 L scale, reporting uncommon virtue, and predicting police performance. *Psychological Services, 10*(1), 123–130. doi:10.1037/a0029062

Weiss, P. A., & Weiss, W. U. (2011). Criterion-related validity in police psychological evaluations. In J. Kitaeff (Ed.), *Series in applied psychology. Handbook of police psychology* (pp. 125–133). New York, NY: Routledge/Taylor & Francis Group.

Woods v. Town of Danville, WV, 712 F. Supp. 2d 502 (2010).

10

CONCLUSION

LEARNING OBJECTIVES

- Identify the key factor to consider when using a psychological test to make an important decision

- Describe what it means when a test has strong psychometric support

- Describe two situations in which using a psychological test that is not reliable can cause harm

- Discuss the challenges of making a good psychological test

- Describe two controversies about using psychological tests for decision making

- Identify two reasons that psychologists continue to use revised versions of tests developed many years ago

- Describe changes to psychological testing we might see in the future

In the previous chapters, we looked at how psychological tests are used in hiring police officers, conducting research on temper tantrums, informing policy in public education, and determining the fate of a small group of inmates on death row. We also examined how psychological tests are used prior to accepting patients for gastric bypass surgery and in the treatment of mental health problems. These are some examples of how psychological tests have an impact on our daily lives, and there are many more.

THE IMPORTANCE OF PSYCHOMETRICS

Across all of these examples, there is one key issue. Tests that are used in real-life situations, those that affect the lives of test takers or have an impact on important decisions, must have strong psychometric support. This means that the test must have documented reliability so it approximates a true score, and it must have documented validity for the purpose for which it is employed. Chapter 2 discusses these concepts and explains how test developers demonstrate the reliability and validity of psychological tests.

A clinician might find a test online that seems like it provides a measure of autistic features in adults. If the clinician does not examine the test closely to find out if it is a reliable test and to determine whether any research has shown it to accurately measure autistic features in adults, he might be misled by test results. Treatment of his client could be misguided, and his client, and her family, would suffer. The test developer in this hypothetical situation may have prepared a checklist of features based on her experience and provided a cutoff score that made sense to her. Much like the emotional sensitivity test discussed in Chapter 2, the autism test would be based on one person's experience. It might be a good test, but it might not. Until research is done to examine its psychometric qualities, the test should not be used in real-life situations.

Similarly, if a test is administered to job applicants with a goal of selecting the best candidate and the test is not reliable or not valid for the purpose of selecting candidates, some applicants who would have been good employees will be denied a position and poorer candidates will be offered jobs. In the most high-stakes situations, using tests that do not have good psychometric support can result in making poorly informed, life-changing decisions, up to and including whether an offender should be spared the death penalty.

THE CHALLENGES IN DEVELOPING GOOD TESTS

Another important issue that becomes apparent when thinking about the examples in this text is the challenge of test development. Not one of the tests discussed provides a perfect measure of anything. That includes the most well researched, best supported tests such as the MMPI-2 and WAIS-IV. Why not? Human attributes are hard to define and even harder to measure. We can only approximate and we can never know with certainty a true score on a psychological test. In researching the validity of a test, we can only compare test results to those of similar tests or to behaviors or outcomes that are imperfectly connected to test results. Perhaps results are being compared to results of lab studies that don't perfectly generalize to real-world situations, or perhaps they are being compared to real-life outcomes that are impacted by a lot of different variables that are not under the control of the researchers. This situation was explored in Chapter 9, in reviewing the challenges in conducting research on the use of psychological tests in selecting police officers.

CONTROVERSIES ABOUT PSYCHOLOGICAL TESTING

We also examined some of the controversies, the differing opinions among psychologists, about using psychological tests in real-world settings. Some psychologists question the presence of personality traits that transcend situations. If personality traits don't carry over to different situations, why measure them at all? Some question the validity of psychological tests, suggesting that tests cannot measure the attributes they are designed to measure with sufficient accuracy to be used in decision making. They believe that there is not enough evidence to indicate that test results predict outcome, such as in testing prior to bariatric surgery, so that it would be unethical to use test results to determine who is allowed to have the surgery. Similarly, some psychologists believe that it is unethical to rely on psychological test results to make recommendations about parenting plans in child custody disputes because there is not enough evidence to indicate that test results are predictive of behaviors relevant to competent parenting.

Other psychologists might argue that information about people needs to be gathered and decisions need to be made, even if tests provide imperfect measures of the relevant attributes and even if those attributes imperfectly predict behavior and outcomes. They would argue that test results contribute to better decisions than would be made without them, and they contribute to better outcomes. This is a researchable hypothesis. Researchers would first have to define a good outcome and decide how to measure it, and those decisions would surely be controversial as well.

THE PAST AND FUTURE OF PSYCHOLOGICAL TESTING

As noted in Chapter 5, some of the most frequently used tests in psychology are revisions of tests developed in the first half of the 20th century. It takes a long time to develop and validate new tests to use in high-stakes decision making, and revisions of tried and true psychological tests such as the MMPI-2 and the Wechsler tests of intellectual functioning are trusted by psychologists and are widely used in a broad variety of applications.

The near and certainly far future will bring a range of new measurement tools and ways of using them. In mental health treatment, in the not too distant future, we may see more routine monitoring of treatment progress and outcome, a more widespread use of the therapeutic assessment model of treatment, and better validated performance-based, or projective, measures. In education, there is likely to be more computerized adaptive testing, a form of testing that uses statistical tools to match item difficulty to the test taker's ability.

Psychologists who work on selecting employees and developing talent for organizations are already using new approaches to measurement, such as gaming technology and mobile devices, and they are also measuring traits, such as the *dark side* of personality (e.g, Hogan Development Survey, www.hoganassessments .com), which were previously neglected. These psychologists, known as industrial-organizational psychologists, could be at the forefront of finding new ways of measuring human attributes for the purpose of predicting behavior. The corporations they work for are motivated to find cost-effective methods of gaining competitive advantages through hiring the right people and developing their talents and skills. They might seek out the innovative work of entrepreneurs in the field to reach that goal.

Although it is still common to administer core psychological tests via paper and pencil, computer assisted administration, scoring, and interpretation of tests is increasingly popular among psychologists. One question that psychologists are asking is whether an IQ test can be wholly administered by computer, without human observation or interaction. Some authors speculate that this will be possible in the near future (Vrana & Vrana, 2017).

Mobile devices, such as smartphones, have been used for several years to record different kinds of experiences. For example, a smartphone can be used to monitor mood at regular or random intervals (see Dubad, Winsper, Meyer, Livanou, & Marwaha, 2017). In some applications that use smartphones to collect data, clients enter data themselves. However, in a recent application, client functioning is monitored unobtrusively with smartphone sensors (Ben-Zeev et al., 2017). Collecting data unobtrusively on a smartphone would not meet the definition of psychological testing on its own, but combined with other approaches to measurement, it could offer new ways to examine self-awareness and other important aspects of human functioning.

Finally, there are always new characteristics to measure or to measure better. Over 4,500 tests were added to the PsycTests database in 2016 alone. This database is published by the American Psychological Association and is primarily intended to be used by scientists in search of psychological tests to use in their research. Over 46,000 tests are in the database and more are added every day.

KEY TAKEAWAYS

There are always going to be new and refined measurement tools and methods of analyzing data, and there will always be controversies about using psychological tests. However, a few key principles are likely to remain important as decision makers and problem solvers think about how to use psychological tests to help them in their work:

- No matter how advanced the technology and methods of measurement, it will be essential to ensure that psychological tests used in everyday life have strong psychometric foundations. Only then can test users have confidence that a test provides accurate data, and only when it provides accurate data can a test contribute to effective decision making.

- A test score approximates a true score and allows the user to make inferences about underlying attributes. Psychological tests don't measure attributes directly.

- The interpretation of a test score can be influenced by politics, social policies, and legal actions. This was made clear in the chapter considering intellectual disability and the death penalty. Similar test scores have been interpreted differently in death penalty cases, resulting in starkly different outcomes.

- In many circumstances, tests should not be the sole source of information relied on when making important decisions. For example, in clinical settings, test scores should be a part of a more thorough assessment. A high score on the BDI-II is an important piece of information to consider in understanding a client and thinking about his or her needs, but it should not be used on its own to determine if a client has a depressive disorder.

- Technical challenges in test development require thoughtful and creative solutions in statistical methods and research design. Some examples of technical challenges are identifying appropriate cutoff scores for unique populations, such as bariatric surgery candidates, and conducting validation studies when public safety and ethical concerns limit research possibilities, as they do for research on selecting police officers.

- Psychological tests can harm as well as help people. Legal constraints are placed on their use to protect vulnerable populations in some circumstances, such as when tests are used in employee selection. Scientists face limits in the tests they use through the peer-review process and also because of the need for approval from an institutional review board before conducting experiments involving people. Other practitioners follow the ethical guidelines of their professions when making decisions about a testing program.

- Testing for child custody evaluation in high conflict divorce, as discussed in Chapter 7, provides a good example of how tests are used along with other information to answer carefully formulated questions. Psychological tests are most helpful when they are used thoughtfully, keeping in mind the purpose of testing in a given circumstance as well as the strengths and limitations of tests in achieving one's goals.

Discussion Questions

1. Chapter 3 is concerned with education testing on an international scale and discusses how test results inform national education policies. Imagine if testing in other arenas was done in a similar way and to meet a similar goal, that is, to influence national policies. What might we be able to learn?

2. Imagine you are responsible for employee selection for an innovative business in the technology sector. Would you use psychological tests in the hiring process?

    What would you want to find out? What new technologies could you use?

3. Think about some of your own experiences of taking psychological tests. What were they like for you? What did you think of the results? Having read the text, do you understand your experiences any differently?

4. Do you think you will be administering tests or devising a testing program in your professional career? If so, what issues are likely to be important in your field?

Research Ideas

1. Conduct a survey to find out what kinds of experiences people in your community have had with psychological testing, whether as test taker, family member of a test taker, or test administrator. What are their thoughts and feelings about their experiences?

2. Examine how tests are used by elementary school classroom teachers. How do teachers make decisions about their testing practices?

    What different kinds of tests do they use? What do they learn about their students from testing? What are their opinions about testing?

3. What psychometric studies have been conducted in support of the use of games for employee selection? What are some of the challenges in further development of these kinds of tests?

References

Ben-Zeev, D., Brian, R., Wang, R., Wang, W., Campbell, A. T., Aung, M. S., . . . & Scherer, E. A. (2017, April). CrossCheck: Integrating self-report, behavioral sensing, and smartphone use to identify digital indicators of psychotic relapse. *Psychiatric Rehabilitation Journal*, *40*(3), 266–275. Retrieved from http://dx.doi.org/10.1037/prj0000243

Dubad, M., Winsper, C., Meyer, C., Livanou, M., & Marwaha, S. (2017, June). A systematic review of the psychometric properties, usability, and clinical impacts of mobile mood-monitoring applications in young people. *Psychological Medicine*, 1–21. Retrieved from http://dx.doi.org/10.1017/S0033291717001659

Vrana, S. R., & Vrana, D. T. (2017, June). Can a computer administer a Wechsler intelligence test? *Research and Practice*, *48*(3), 191–198. Retrieved from http://dx.doi.org/10.1037/pro0000128

INDEX